#opioidCRISIS
THE REALITY OF ADDICTION

#opioidCRISIS
THE REALITY OF ADDICTION

WHAT TO DO AND
HOW TO HELP

Rev. Charles F. Plauché

ISBN: 978-1-949639-58-2
LCCN: 2019939708

*This book is dedicated to all those who are still suffering
and the families who love them*

TABLE OF CONTENTS

INTRODUCTION

There's a crisis in America.

All across the country, this crisis is hitting people hard. It does not discriminate by age, race, economic status, gender, or politics; it is harming and killing people from all walks of life. It is a crisis that seemed to come on fast—in some cases out of nowhere—and it is devastating entire communities. You probably have heard about it, and chances are, your life has been touched by it. But if you are like millions of other people, even as you watch a loved one suffer, you don't know what to do or how to help.

I'm speaking, of course, about the opioid epidemic that has come to the forefront of our national consciousness in recent years. But despite appearances, this crisis is not as new as it seems, and when you put it into the context of drug and alcohol abuse, it's not new at all. The opioid crisis is just the most recent, terrifying chapter in a larger story of addiction, one that is all too familiar to many American families.

Addiction has destroyed so many lives. Countless articles, news stories, and television shows have documented how drugs and alcohol can drive a promising and hopeful life right off the edge of a cliff. Yet, despite an overwhelming amount of discussion, people still have no idea where to turn for help. They don't know what kind of help is available and they don't really know what help is. Sometimes the so-called help that people find only serves to prolong the problem, or make it worse.

That's why I'm writing this book. As the Executive Director of Haven House Addiction Recovery, a nonprofit organization established to provide long-term highly controlled and structured support for men in recovery, I have spent years coming face to face with the causes, devastation, and aftermath of addiction. I've seen enough hard cases and witnessed enough transformations to know that with hard work, dedication, and a willingness to change, there is a path to recovery. I should know—I've been through it myself.

MY STORY

I come from a happy, middle-class family. Growing up, we had everything in the world. Mom was loving and attentive; Dad was always home for dinner; we always had food on the table and a roof over our head. It was sort of like *Leave It to Beaver*. But for some reason, I never felt as though I really fit in—something was always missing. I couldn't explain it except to say that I just wasn't comfortable in my own skin.

Then, one day when I was thirteen, I was sitting in my older brother's Gran Torino—I loved that car—and found a flask of scotch. I took a sip of it, and the moment the warmth from that alcohol hit me, I thought, This is what I've been missing. I drank the whole thing.

From there my struggle began. For me, alcohol was the only thing that made me feel normal—like I finally fit in. As long as I could have a drink "just a little bit," I'd be okay. But from that very first sip in my brother's car, I could never have "just a little bit." I was hooked almost instantly, and I drank to excess every time.

My spiral downward began immediately as well. By fourteen I was drunk all the time. By fifteen I was driving, wrecking cars, and getting busted for driving under the influence. Not knowing what to do, my family began their own journey of enabling me. They bailed me out, made excuses, and financed my addiction. All of their covering for me gave me a license to continue down my destructive path. When they started to back away, or challenge me and my behavior, I manipulated them back to being on my side. I lied to them, stole from them, guilt-tripped them—whatever it took to get what I wanted. And as long as they played along, I had no reason to stop.

I drank and I drank, and the whole time I would deny that I was drinking too much. When it became too much to deny, I tried to normalize it. Everybody gets a DUI every now and then; everybody drinks until they black out sometimes. I wasn't just lying to everyone else, I was lying to myself, and I was buying it all—hook, line, and sinker.

I managed to graduate from high school and even go to college, but the destructive behavior continued. It didn't matter how many times the judge said, "I'm going to put you in jail," or how many times a woman said, "I'm going to leave you." It didn't matter how many times my parents told me, "You do it again, and we're going to disown you." Like all drug addicts and alcoholics, I had full faith in my ability to manipulate anyone in my path, and nothing was more important to me than my next drink.

Years passed like this, and the drinking got worse. I went from place to place, job to job, relationship to relationship. When I could no longer manipulate someone or they wouldn't cosign on my destructive life, I would move on to the next boss, friend, girlfriend, or whoever.

Finally, I was so miserable, I couldn't take any more. I called my father and said, "I've had enough. What do I do?" My father said, "Come on back home." Off to a treatment facility I went.

Of course, in many ways, that was just the beginning. I struggled through treatment, in and out, but when things finally clicked, I realized it was my calling to devote my life to service.

It happened when I read something in a book: a person could have a happy and joyous life if he could just devote his life to others. At that moment I had a vision, a moment of clarity. I had an instant picture of myself, devoting my life to helping others, and having a happy, wonderful life. In the same moment, I had a clear vision of my life if I did not do this, and it was a life of turmoil and despair. I had heard the voice of God, and I knew which future I wanted to claim.

I have devoted my life to service ever since.

HOW IS AN ADDICT MADE?

My story is not unique. Scratch the surface of any family and you will find someone dealing with the cycle of addiction. But how can you tell if a person's substance abuse is an actual addiction? How can you differentiate between a bad habit, the folly of youth, a rough spell, and a full-blown addiction?

Chances are, if you are reading this book, you are concerned that you, or someone you love, is an addict. And if you are concerned enough to be reading this book, chances are, you're right. It's important to trust your gut. If you've seen someone jeopardize relationships, jobs, and health due to substance abuse, you're probably dealing with an addict.

You might be wondering, How did they become an addict? Was it something I did? Were they just born this way? Is this the result of nurture or nature? And the answer is yes.

You can tell by looking at a family tree that there is certainly a genetic predisposition to addiction. Great-Grandpa, Grandpa, and Dad were all alcoholics, and now Junior is struggling with heroin. I see it running through families every single day.

You can also tell by observing communities and neighborhoods where drug epidemics flourish that it's also environmental, reflecting local culture and rituals, socioeconomics, peer pressure, or any of a host of reasons. Anyone who works with people in recovery can see that addiction has roots in both genetics and environment.

No matter what the reason, origin, or specifics of the situation, the cycle of addiction remains consistent. At first, it's not a big deal. An addict will use alcohol or drugs recreationally, or on occasion. But because of their genetic makeup, environment, or a combination of both, they quickly lose control of the situation. That loss of control leads to more frequent use, in larger amounts.

Pretty soon, they are lying, cheating, and manipulating everyone around them so they can continue their substance abuse. This leads to devastating guilt and shame. The only thing that can quiet that guilt is to drink more or do drugs again. After a while, they need to have a buzz on all the time just to get through the day.

Then, paranoia sets in as people begin to worry. Will they find out? Who knows what? Folks report that they can't sleep; they're afraid somebody will find out something and they won't be there to defend themselves or lie their way out of it. All of which, of course, leads them to rely even more heavily on the drugs and alcohol. And on it goes, until the substance abuse has taken everything from them and ruined their lives.

Every situation is as unique as the individual who is struggling. But every cycle of addiction is the same:

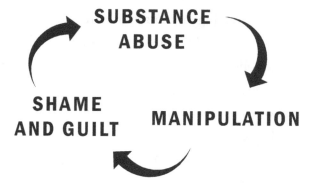

People may not be born manipulators, but addicts become very good at it, very quickly. The average person doesn't walk through life lying, and they don't assume anyone else is lying either. That makes them an easy target for manipulation, especially in the early stages of addiction. Regular, average folks will give you the benefit of the doubt a hundred times. Pretty soon, addicts are lying their way out of every situation:

"Hey, look, I'm missing money out of my wallet. Did you take it?"

"Absolutely not."

"But we're the only two people here."

"I don't know. Maybe you lost it."

"No, I swear it was here last night. Now it's gone."

"Maybe you miscounted. I didn't take it. Let me help you find it."

Addicts are adept at making the people who love them doubt themselves, causing everyone around them to think they're the crazy ones. Eventually, people start catching on to the lies, but now they can't follow through on consequences. Threats are usually idle. "If you ever do it again . . ." means nothing. After that first idle threat, an addict begins to believe all threats are idle.

Eventually, parents and spouses end up not just believing lies, not just failing to follow through on threats, but enabling the lifestyle. They are manipulated into paying fines, paying rent, paying light bills. They give the addict money for their car payment or food— money that ends up going to pay for the drugs. Addicts will promise, "I'll quit. I will never do it again," but it's just another lie. Everyone knows it at that point, but now the whole family is as sick as the addict.

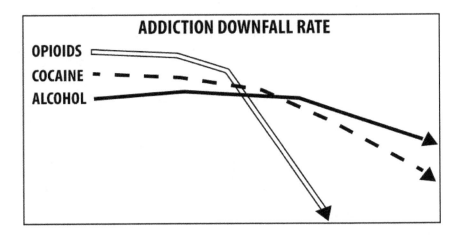

While the root causes and the path of addiction are the same no matter what the substance, the opioid crisis is unique in some terrible ways. The downfall is exponentially faster. Jobs and relationships come apart very quickly. The illegality and cost lead to more criminal behavior. Detox is a nightmare, even if you're only doing small amounts. Withdrawals will start after your very first use, and they will hit far harder than a bad hangover. When you're coming off of opioids, you wish to die, but you won't. The effect on your physiology is devastating, and it is a much faster decline.

There are some significant differences between being addicted to alcohol and being addicted to drugs, and we're seeing them as drug addiction rolls through and devastates whole communities. We're all acutely aware of the drug "problem."

So how do we solve this problem? Outlawing the substance doesn't solve it. I'm not saying drugs should be easy to get, but you're not going to stop drug use this way. Locking people up doesn't solve it either. You can jail an addict for a year, and as soon as he is released, the first thing he'll do is find drugs. You cannot reason with an addict. Explaining to them how much damage heroin does to their body won't make a bit of difference. Because in the end, we're not dealing with a drug problem, or an alcohol problem. The problem we're dealing with is spiritual, and it requires a spiritual solution.

In this way, the treatment of alcohol addiction and opioid addiction can be approached in the same way. It doesn't matter where an addict is from, how old he is, or what he's addicted to—the solution will always be spiritual.

Take Justin, for example the Program Director of Haven House Addiction Recovery. He also went through our program. Like me, Justin comes from a good family; his dad's a well-known and respected member of the community, he has a loving and devoted mother, and his brother is a first responder whom everybody knows and loves. Justin is a nice guy with a good upbringing, a sharp mind, and a lot of potential. Yet he found himself spiraling down the drain of opioids, using his vast capabilities to deceive, manipulate, and thieve, all in the hopes of scoring more drugs. When he came to us, he was in a desperate situation, and I wasn't sure he would make it. We are so grateful that he did, not only for his sake, but because he has proven himself invaluable to Haven House—a men-only facility, for reasons we'll discuss later—and the men in our care.

Throughout this book, I will refer to Justin's story, sometimes in his own words, to give the perspective of someone who went through recovery for opioid addiction. It was difficult for him, just as it was for me. But he has benefitted from Haven House's philosophy and focus on the spiritual problem that lies at the heart of the issue.

THE INSIDE JOB

One thing that every drug addict has in common is that an addict will put their addiction at the center of their own spiritual life, replacing God. If you've taken God's place at the center of your universe, that means you believe that you are the arbiter of truth, you have the answers to everything, and the world revolves around you.

This is exactly how addicts think—and exactly how they treat the people they love. They're egocentric. Everything is about them, and they don't care whose lives they destroy. If you are the center of your own universe, then everyone else is just there for your use and abuse. Addicts lose both the concept of other people's feelings and their interpersonal relationship skills. Everyone is just there to support their insanity, and when people refuse to play along, they are discarded for someone who will. This is why I always tell our fellows, "You don't have girlfriends and wives. You take women hostage."

During the twelve-month residential program at Haven House, we offer more than just abstinence from drugs and alcohol. We help men put God back into the center of their lives and teach them to rely on His power and strength. We provide them with structure and

9

order in their day-to-day so they can find structure and order in their minds. We help them find a spiritual connection that will allow them to put others first.

What we're dealing with is not drug use, but a person's inner being. This is an inside job. The alcohol and drugs are just symptoms of the larger disease. If you have psoriasis and just rub a little ointment on it, it's going to feel better, but it's not going away. The cause is inside your body. It's the same thing with alcohol and drugs, but instead of the skin, it's a malady of the heart. Healing someone's heart is much harder than taking away drugs and alcohol, and that's why so many addicts don't make it.

Success in recovery relies on an addict's willingness to change. You'll often hear about people hitting rock bottom before going to treatment. But the truth is, even after they've reached that point, it will not be easy.

When I decided to seek treatment for my alcohol addiction, I'd had enough, and I was desperate for a change. Still, I fought it the whole way. Despite everything in my world falling apart, I just couldn't believe that they were right about me. I had to be different. I often say I was terminally unique. My ego was so out of control that even though I knew they were right, I couldn't admit it. If they were right, it meant one thing to me: it meant I was wrong, and that everything I had been doing and saying for so many years was wrong too.

I already knew it was wrong, but seeking treatment meant having to admit it. The devastation and the destruction I had caused, the times I had stolen from my family, the worry I had caused them, the money they had spent on my behalf—I would have to own up to all of it. I couldn't blame anybody else anymore. There were many times it all felt too hard. Many times I wanted to quit. But I was done with the addict lifestyle. My desire for change kept me on the right path until I let God back in to the center of my life and let Him take over.

It can't just be the addict who is willing to change. Everyone in the family has to find that desire—and stick with it. We deal with families all the time who say they are willing to do what it takes, and they mean it when they say it. But when push comes to shove, they just can't do it. They get sucked back in. The family dynamic is warped, and if they are not committed to doing their own work, to examining their own behaviors and lives, they'll be pulled back into making excuses and paving the way for more destruction.

ABOUT THIS BOOK

That brings us to you. If you're reading this book, and you've gotten this far—if these stories of lying and manipulation sound familiar, if you're seeing devastation and destruction in your life or the life of your loved one, there's a good chance you're dealing with an addict.

This book will help you understand the nature of addiction and what you can do to fight it. In this book, I will talk about the cycle of addiction and:

- how it impacts the life of the addict and those around them;

- the ways in which loved ones can do more damage, and the ways in which they can help;

- the cycle of recovery;

- the Haven House approach to Christ-centered treatment; and

- what steps you can take next.

After dealing with an addict for so many years, through so many crises and so much manipulation, you might be thinking, This is a hopeless situation. This is just the way it is.

I'm here to tell you: it's not hopeless. There is a path to recovery. The road is long and there are hard choices and difficult realities along the way. This book will not offer you a cure or a simple solution—because there are no cures, and there are no simple solutions. But there is hope, and informing yourself is an important and powerful first step toward a healthy, happy, drug- and alcohol-free life for you and your loved ones.

CHAPTER 1

STAGES OF ADDICTION

Although addiction to alcohol and addiction to drugs have some superficial differences, both tend to follow the same path. Addicts might think of themselves as unique and special, but the stages of addiction are not that different from person to person. In this chapter I am going to review the basic stages of addiction to help you identify what you might be experiencing or witnessing.

For the purposes of this book, I am going to talk about addiction in three stages:

1) social,

2) dependent, and

3) addictive.

These stages don't always happen in an exact order, or for a specific amount of time. Addiction won't neatly progress from one stage to another like a caterpillar to a butterfly (and it certainly won't be as pretty). People might experience a stage in one day. They might live in a stage for years. They might experience two stages simultaneously. But just because you might see these ebb and flow, or happen at different speeds, you're still seeing someone progress through the stages of addiction.

THE SOCIAL STAGE

The social stage is often hard to spot. During this stage, addicts might look like everyone else when they party with friends. Things for addicts don't look so bad. They're really not getting in any trouble. There are no financial problems. They're not having problems at work or with family. They're just going out for drinks with friends, or doing drugs at a party. They might look like an average person blowing off steam, reaching for adulthood, celebrating something, or just having a good time.

What you can't see is that, for the addict, it feels different—like they have finally found something that helps them feel normal. They might be finding acceptance from a group for the first time. Their inhibitions have dropped a little and now they can get outside of themselves so they're a little more social, a little more outgoing.

Justin, our Program Director I mentioned earlier, was sixteen and had already been drinking socially for a few years when he started experimenting with marijuana and mushrooms.

"Looking back now, knowing what an addict is, I still wouldn't have identified myself as having a problem," he says of that time. But when he was seventeen, he moved to a different town and started at a new school, and the change triggered social anxiety.

"I remember drinking one particular time, getting drunk, and thinking to myself, 'Oh man, this is it. This was the best thing ever—this is the cure for everything.'"

For an addict, the substance makes any kind of anxiety or insecurity go away. It shuts out immediate problems, or at least allows the user to change the way they feel about themselves at the time.

"I still wasn't drinking every weekend," says Justin. "I was mostly drinking at parties, just a little bit more."

PREDISPOSITION

The social stage is especially hard for people who are predisposed to addiction. A person with a family history of addiction, trauma in their past, or other environmental causes for dependency won't often stay in the social stage for very long.

Some people live in the social stage and never become addicted. They enjoy alcohol, but don't need it to come out of their shell. Or, when they are drinking too much, they realize that there's an issue. They overdo it one time, and the hangover serves as their punishment and warning.

But people who are predisposed can't stop after they drink too much. They can't stop after they embarrass themselves, or have a horrible hangover, or put lives at risk by driving drunk. They don't learn a lesson because the effect of the chemical is too life-changing. Their long-term need to fit in, and the discovery of something that allows for that, are just too important.

For some people, the social stage will be incredibly brief. They'll have that drink and almost immediately move to the dependent stage. It won't take more than a week or two before they begin to use and drink like an addict. People who go through this stage slowly will begin to rationalize. The problems will start small and appear gradually, so they will justify them, put them aside, and try to cover them:

Mother: "Did you leave your keys in the door when you came home last night?"

Addict Son: "Yes, I was so tired."

Mother: "Were you high again?"

Addict Son: "I was fine when I got home, just really sleepy."

SHIFTING FROM SOCIAL TO DEPENDENT

In the social stage, a person can still choose when to drink and when not to, and the impact on their lives won't be long lasting or severe. When people start ignoring reasonable warning signs in the social stage, that's when you know something has shifted.

Let's say you're dating someone, and he gets really high, nods out at a dinner party, and embarrasses the heck out of you. The next day you let him know his behavior was unacceptable. He says, "I don't want to lose you. It won't happen again." You love this person, so you trust him.

But then it does happen again. Despite your tears, pleading, and threats, the behavior continues. Now you know he's gone from the social stage to something else. He has to do it again, so he's overlooking the warnings and threats. He's begun to rationalize that you're just an old stick in the mud. Now, when he does it again and you complain, he'll try to make it your fault. He'll tell you you've got to loosen up, that this is what everyone does. He deflects the threat, and he says he's tired of your nagging and if you don't leave him alone , you're going to lose him.

STAGES OF ADDICTION

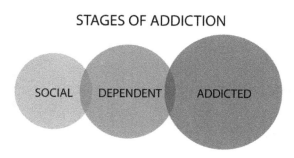

He's flipped the script, leaving you devastated, angry, and more than a little confused. That's because eventually addicts will begin to prioritize the substance above everyone else in their life, including loved ones.

THE DEPENDENT STAGE

After the social stage, whether it lasts for one day or ten years, an addict will move into the dependent stage. In this stage addicts will begin to form habits around how, when, and where they get high. They will need more and more to achieve the feeling they used to get from using, and the drugs will take precedence over their jobs, their health, and even their family. Soon, nothing will stand between them and their drugs, even if it means lying, cheating, or stealing from the people who love them.

RITUALS

Something that every addict has in common is the development of rituals. The ritual is the formation of habits surrounding the substance use. Though every addict's ritual is as unique as they are, it is always about obsession. So, you might be at work, but all you can think about from the moment you get there is the ritual: what you're going to drink, or what drug you're going to do, where you're going to do it, how you're going to do it, and who you're going to do it with. The obsession with the drug haunts you all day, so at the end of the day, no matter what else is happening, you are going to follow through with that ritual.

What does a ritual look like? For intravenous drug users, it's a certain rig, a certain strap. They like to inject it into a certain part of their body, watching the drug be drawn into the needle and then plunged into their vein. Someone who snorts a drug will have a whole plan for how they are going to do that: First, I'll crush it with this particular pencil, or I'll use the bottom of this glass, and then I'll use the new spoon that I just bought . . .

REV. CHARLES F. PLAUCHÉ

When I drank, my ritual involved a certain brand of bourbon, with a certain shape of ice cube, for which I had a particular tray. I had a very special glass I loved to drink from—I can remember when I found it, but I was really excited about it, and I protected it assiduously.

The thought process behind rituals is specific, obsessive, and wrongheaded. If everything's right—the right glass, the right brand, the right needle, or the right vein—if it's all set up nice and neat, and not haphazardly, then it is going to be a wonderful high. Nothing bad will happen because you've done everything properly.

Whatever ritual addicts have built up in their minds, they have dreamed about doing it all day. They believe it will provide them with their best high and that the experience will be rewarding. After putting all of that thought and energy into the ritual, nothing can stop them from following through on it.

We worked with an alcoholic whom we'll call Carl, and like me, he had a glass that he loved. He loved it so much, that once when he was out helping a friend shop for a car, he ended up buying one for himself—because his glass fit perfectly in the cup holder.

He said the car was beautiful, brand new with a red leather interior. But he admitted that none of that mattered. He bought it because his cocktail glass fit nicely in the cup holder, and that was the priority. It would become part of his ritual, and that's why he had to have it. Never mind that in this case the ritual meant driving while intoxicated—the ritual becomes such a priority in the life of the addict that it borders on OCD-like behavior.

COMPULSION

When the compulsion kicks in, there's no denying it anymore. If dinner plans with your girlfriend threaten to get in the way of your ritual, then you have to find a way to avoid it. You'll pick a fight so that she will cancel it, because following through with your plan is more important than spending time with her.

Here's the kind of story we hear all the time: An intravenous-opioid user is at his sister's wedding. After a while, maybe from watching people drinking, or just from being kept from his drug for so long, he can't stand it anymore, so he tells someone, "I gotta go to the bathroom, I'll be right back." And then he disappears for five days.

One fellow we worked with was in court for a child custody hearing in Alabama. He tried to stay clean because he knew getting his children depended on it, but the obsession was plaguing him terribly. It got so bad that during the hearing, he actually left the courtroom, went to the restroom, shot up in his left arm, and came back in to see the judge with blood on his sleeve—high as a kite. Needless to say, he lost his children, as he should have.[1]

Every addict, or loved one of an addict, will recognize this behavior. It is deeply frustrating and hard for a healthy person to understand, but once the compulsion is in place, it is impossible for the addict to stop the behavior without serious help. That's why when someone arrives at Haven House, the first thing we seek to do is replace their rituals. We are up at six o'clock in the morning for prayer and meditation, and we go until nine or ten at night. We have meetings and classes before work, then meetings and classes after work, keeping them busy until lights out. In this way, we replace damaging drug rituals with positive rituals involving work, prayer, hygiene, and personal responsibility.

It may seem like a small thing, but this is why we have our guys make their bed every day. It's a requirement: wake up and make your

---

1. I ended up in court with him later, after he had been through our program. He did get his children back then, and he is doing great today.

bed. For some of them it's a habit that replaces the first needle of the day, or the first swig from a flask. When they go on their first home visit, the parents call and say, "What have you done to him? He's making the bed, for God's sake." It's a simple ritual, but they do it every day—as do I. It's a first step to establishing a new life.

PHYSICAL DEPENDENCY

During the dependent stage, chemical dependency increases, and as it does, so does consumption. As addicts' tolerance increases, they need larger quantities as they chase that feeling of euphoria from their first high. As they consume more, their behavior changes. Hangovers and withdrawal worsen, causing people to sweat, shake uncontrollably, vomit. It's basically agony until they can get high again.

This is especially true for opioid users. Justin described his first physical withdrawal from opiates, which was so bad, even after years of addiction, he never forgot it:

> I wanted to die. You can't die but you want to die. You feel like you have an endless, horrible flu, with aches and pains, sleeplessness, chills, and upset stomach. When I say sleeplessness, I mean you do not sleep. You can't. Your body is so used to having that numbing drug that dulls all your senses, so suddenly everything is awake and on fire. It's like you're on high alert. Every nerve ending is active—if somebody touches you, you get chills. Your hair's sticking up on end constantly. A breeze hits you, your skin goes crazy. Eventually somebody comes through with some pills and you take some more of them, so the sickness goes away. Then you're riding that until all the pills run out, and it just starts this cycle. I was in that cycle for years. A few months of feeling great, having plenty of pills and drugs, and then **boom**, out of pills. Dope sick.

At the same time, emotional pain is increasing too. Misery and guilt are compounded with panic as blackouts, memory loss, or bizarre behavior become more common. (I once found myself in Las Vegas at a blackjack table, with no recollection of how I'd gotten there.) All of this contributes to a sense of being unwell, crazy, and unstable. Your self-esteem suffers. Eventually, the emotional misery can be more painful than the physical.

The cost of being addicted keeps climbing, both literally and figuratively. The monetary cost isn't the worst part, at least in the beginning. The physical and emotional tolls and how they affect your relationships are more severe. The truth is, everyone in your life ends up paying for your habit, one way or another.

There's no set formula to measure an increase in consumption. It's not as simple as a gallon of whiskey versus a pint, or one hit from a crack pipe versus seven. Everybody has different tolerances and different breaking points. One person may be up to a case of beer a day, another person might be doing half that amount, but the result is the same.

I quantify the progression of dependency by the destruction of relationships. Eventually the addict will lose control. The euphoric, fun, and exciting feelings that came with getting drunk or high are gone now, unachievable—but they still can't stop. The goal has shifted to straight intoxication.

THE ADDICTIVE STAGE

As they enter the addictive stage, people in addicts' lives might start telling them, "You have a problem." But the addict has decided that the chemicals are the only thing they can count on or believe in. They'll tell themselves things like, "The boss is mean. People don't really love me. Nobody understands me. Nobody treats me right. Nobody listens. Only the chemicals are my friend. When I use, I can trust it and I feel good about it."

Addicts exist in a prison of their own making. Biblically speaking, we talk about being in bondage, and that's what this stage is: total bondage to chemicals. The Bible talks about being a slave to one thing or another—money, sex, drugs, or any number of things—and how only when you are a slave to God are you truly free. I call that freedom through servitude.

Justin recalls doing whatever he needed to get pills, from doctor shopping, to coordinating schedules with fellow addicts for prescriptions, to stealing from his grandparents:

> *I had to make sure not to run out of pills, because if I ran out of pills people would find out because I looked like hell. I couldn't function at work. I couldn't be around my family because they knew something was wrong. I couldn't be around my girlfriend because she thought I had quit. I told everybody I quit, that I was doing better, and they would all be disappointed. It's high stress that you put on yourself on top of being dope sick, on top of needing money because these pills are expensive. It's a very chaotic life.*

The euphoria of drug use is gone—it's just a memory that you're chasing now. You start rationalizing: I'm not going to do much. I'm just going to have one hit. I'm just going to do one pill. I'm only going to snort it tonight. I'm not going to inject it because that way, I'll just get that nice little buzz and I won't overdo it today. Everything is going to be different this time.

That's full-blown addiction: being face to face with it, and still denying the problem. We blame others. We rationalize. We project our responsibility onto whoever we can, because having to admit we have a problem would kill us. That false pride and ego represent the idealized version of ourselves that we show people.

IDEALIZED VERSION OF OURSELVES

In this stage, it becomes harder for an addict to function in normal life. They get to work late, leave early, don't talk, don't contribute, mess up projects, represent the company poorly. Eventually they're missing days, even weeks of work, and the excuses are getting old and repetitive.

Finally, when they're fired, they'll say, "This place will fall apart without me. I'm the only one holding it together," when the reality is the opposite. But they still believe they are God's gift to their boss, or to the families that they've torn apart. They believe that they are God's gift to their romantic partners, even though they're not really in relationships, but holding people hostage. They continue to hold a very high opinion of themselves. While they might have been very good workers, spouses, parents, and friends when they were sober, the drugs have made them completely unreliable and dangerous.

The idealized version of ourselves is not limited to the addict. I've got one. You've got one. Everybody has one. But while the average person's idealized version of himself or herself is slightly enhanced, a drug addict's is completely unrealistic.

Drug addicts and alcoholics have the answers to everything. Their minds have become so warped, they think that if people would only listen, they can explain why their boss is at fault for the loss of their job; why it's their spouse's issue that is forcing them out of the house. You are overreacting to the fact that they've ended up in jail eight times. If only you would listen, they can explain to you why their behavior is right, and why somebody else is wrong.

Sometimes the men who come through our program are so sure they are in the right, I tell them, "I'm getting rid of Google now that I've got you. You know everything." I can't tell you how many times we have had an expert in our midst.

I'll say, "Okay. Today we're going to paint the outside fence."

Immediately a hand will shoot up. "Oh, I can do that. I'm an amazing painter."

Or I'll say, "I need someone to fix this door."

"I'm a master carpenter. I've fixed a bunch of doors, I can do this myself," someone will say with the utmost confidence.

But inevitably, when we hand over the reins, they don't have the first clue about what they are doing. Addiction warps the mind so much, it makes people believe they can do anything, that they are above everything, and that they know best. They know all and can do all. They are at the center of all things. They in fact are self-centered and self- seeking. Essentially, they've made themselves God. We see evidence of this in every aspect of their lives, from their reticence to stop their substance abuse, to their belief that with no experience they can accomplish tasks, from the simplest, to the highly complex.

At Haven House, we let people face their failures. So, when someone claims they are the expert at something, we let them try and fail. We let them see that they can't do everything and that's okay. In fact, it's essential, because their false pride and idealized version of themselves stand in the way of their recovery.

SEEKING THE LIKE-MINDED

These walls don't come down so easily. Addicts will do what they can to protect themselves from facing this reality, putting forth more lies, innuendos, and subterfuge. When faced with their concrete inability to hang a door straight or paint a fence perfectly after they've claimed to be the expert, they'll explain to their group of peers why we were wrong and how they could really do it. They'll look for other men with idealized senses of self who will agree with them, and they'll seek to form an alliance.

These are human issues—after all, you don't have to be a drug addict to be self-centered, in denial, or just a jerk. But when drugs are involved, our need to be right—to justify, manipulate, and manage— will drive us to ignore the truth and seek out people who will agree with us, no matter what.

People in the addicted stage always have a reason not to get sober. And their inability to do so is usually someone else's fault. These are the skills they have honed during the dependent stage, blaming everyone else in their life for their problems, while simultaneously denying the problem is as bad as everyone says it is.

A person in the addicted stage will no longer want to spend time with "good people," because a person with a moral center is going to find you out immediately. An addict knows how to seek out like-minded people almost instinctually.

One young man in our program came from a very wealthy family. He always had access to the best things in life and had a top-notch education. Yet, when describing him, his mother said, "He's always been a 'bottom feeder.' He's always sought out the lowest of the low, because in that situation his education and background make him feel superior."

The pattern for a drug addict is to get into a relationship, destroy it, and move to another when that person won't cosign on their insanity anymore. Addicts tend to steal everything they can from the household. They'll destroy relationships with their spouses, their children, their parents, their grandparents, etc., and all the while they'll claim it's the other person who is crazy. Then they'll look for someone to agree with them.

BEG, BORROW, AND STEAL

Addicts are thieves, and they will steal from their family, whether it's through outright theft, or through manipulation. Criminal behavior is not always reported in these cases because family members are reluctant to press charges or push the issue. But in the addiction stage, the behavior of the addict becomes more criminal, and starts to move outside of their immediate circle.

Alcohol is legal, so the criminal behavior of alcoholics tends to come later than it does for addicts who use other drugs. But physical abuse, neglect, and drunk driving are all common criminal behaviors among alcoholics.

The slip into crime is faster for drug addicts. Prescription drugs can become very expensive, costing hundreds of dollars a day. Drug addicts will often turn to dealing drugs to keep their habit afloat. As their tolerance increases, they will need to sell more and more, taking bigger and bigger risks.

Heroin is much cheaper than pills, so it becomes attractive to opioid addicts. But now they are so high that they can't get up off the sofa, so how are they supposed to live? Many of them become prostitutes. They steal prescription pads from doctor's offices. They commit fraud and write checks out of grandma's checkbook. They sneak into their neighbor's house at night and steal his TV.

We've gotten calls from desperate parents asking, "How do I get my son put in jail? What can I do?" Eventually, parents are willing to have their children arrested because they'd rather see them go to prison than go to the grave.

ROCK BOTTOM

Sometimes you will hear people speak about hitting "rock bottom." This is when everything is catching up with you—all the professional, personal, and legal fallout is overwhelming. It's the moment when you know you're facing the end, because you've lost your job, your husband kicked you out, you overdosed, you're homeless, or you're in jail. You've hit a low point, and it forces you to look at the truth of your life.

I don't believe in rock bottom in the traditional sense. I think the notion can be misleading and even harmful for people seeking recovery. For one thing, it causes people to wait. They think, "I'm just not there yet, but eventually I will be and I'll wait for that 'rock bottom' epiphany." But the truth is, there is always further to fall. There's more suffering for us, until we die. There's jail, institutions, homelessness, violence, depression. There's no end to how bad things can get. Waiting for the worst to happen is just a stalling tactic that can lead to unnecessary suffering.

The second problem with "rock bottom" is that it creates a false sense of security: Well, now I've hit rock bottom. There's no way it can get any worse, I'm on my way up now. But don't fool yourself. There's no magical change that occurs when things are terrible. There's no low that will prevent you from relapsing. We can be sober five, ten, twenty years and still end up as active addicts again.

As far as I'm concerned, the only way you hit the bottom is to quit digging. There's nothing truly stopping a person from going lower. Free will means there's always room to throw your life away. In the Bible, Paul put it this way: "For when I am weak, I am strong."[2]

---

2. 2 Cor. 12:10.

If we don't recognize who we really are, including our weaknesses, we can never overcome them.

If we believe we've hit rock bottom, then we can't get in touch with our real weaknesses, or face up to the idea that we are capable of doing anything. I am capable of doing the same thing that a serial killer did, or someone lying on the street, comatose from doing drugs. The only thing separating us from the behaviors we consider abhorrent is our willingness to do better. But make no mistake, it is an act of will.

This is also the good news. If facing your addiction and getting help are choices, then they are choices anyone can make, including you and the people you love.

CHAPTER 2

THE DAMAGE OF ADDICTION

Many rock stars have made addiction the subject of their work. Aside from love, it may be the most documented subject in popular music. While drugs are a ubiquitous part of music culture (second only to sex in the trio of hedonism, "sex, drugs, and rock 'n roll", songwriters have not shied away from the horrors and damage drug use inflicts. The music may be catchy, but it's clear from the lyrics that the outcome of drug use is anything but fun.

Addiction wreaks havoc in the lives of users, beginning the very moment they first use, and that havoc continues until they commit themselves to recovery. The longer the substance abuse goes on, the worse the damage is, emotionally, socially, and physically.

MENTAL AND EMOTIONAL DAMAGE

As we discussed previously, addiction often starts because folks don't feel like they fit in. Genetics and socioeconomic considerations aside, in the addict's mind, they became an addict because they were searching for something their whole lives to help fit in. That first time they use, they believe they has finally found what they've been looking for. When the drug use starts, the only thing users are thinking about is how good it makes them feel, how they are finally comfortable in their own skin. It's easy to focus on this at first, because in the social stage they really don't have too many issues—health, legal, or otherwise. Aside from the occasional headache and fatigue from overdoing it, there aren't many physical effects. Socially, people might laugh about what a fool you made of yourself the night before, but it's not a regular occurrence. Legally, the DUIs and thefts haven't kicked in yet.

There is one side effect of addiction that starts right away, and that is the emotional distress. For new addicts, the realization that they love the chemical—and that is the only thing that makes them feel normal—coincides with the realization that they can't control their use of it, and that it could quickly escalate. They're seeing the way it changes them, and that they're beginning to change their behavior and think differently because of it.

Soon, they have to hide their use, and the double life begins. Let's say Joe is an addict in the social stage. When he is out with friends, he is the life of the party—he's never been more confident and engaged. Maybe toward the end of the night he gets a little wobbly, but everyone is still smiling and having a good time, chalking it up to a good party.

So, everything may still seem all right on the outside, but on the inside, for Joe, the turmoil has already begun. Guilt, shame, and obsession are beginning to take up a lot of real estate in Joe's mind. He goes home and thinks, Oh my god, what did I do? What did I say? Who did I offend?

Joe is insecure to begin with. He was uncomfortable with himself before his addiction took hold—he didn't like who he was. When he wakes up the next morning feeling guilty and ashamed, the euphoria that came with getting high is gone. Now when Joe goes back to work or sees his friends and everybody's laughing, he starts to feel panicked; he assumes that everyone is talking about him, that the jig is up.

A normal person might take a bit of good-natured ribbing and own up to their behavior: "I know, I overdid it! Can you keep it down, I have a headache!" But Joe can't laugh at himself—in fact, he can't even admit he's hungover. If he can't avoid people altogether, he'll start to lie. When somebody says, "You look terrible," he'll say, "Yeah I feel bad. I think I've got a cold coming on." The lying starts immediately, because in Joe's head, he knows his use is a bigger deal than just a party. He needs this drug now, and he doesn't want anyone catching on to how important it has become.

You can see the start of the paranoia right away. An addict will constantly worry about who's going to find out, who might discover their secrets, and what they will lose because of it. They begin to think, Why are they all talking about me? or, They don't like me at work. They're after me, and they're going to fire me. They become paranoid about everything because they're hiding so much.

There's an old saying: "A thief believes that everybody steals."[3] A person who lies or constantly tries to mislead you thinks you're doing

---

3 Attributed to American novelist E. W. Howe.

the same to them. In fact, a drug addict will tell you, "Everybody does it. I don't know why you're so mad at me." When you're in it for yourself, you believe everybody else is too. That's a real hindrance to getting clean and sober.

I have a friend who's an ER doctor. He once told me he hated working with the drug addicts and the alcoholics who come through the hospital. When I asked why, he said, "Because I'm trying to save their lives while they're telling me, 'You're just after my money.' And, for the most part, they don't have any money."

Another thing I have often heard over the years, especially from people on probation: "The court system is a money-making scheme. The system is all about the money." They've been driving drunk, lost their children in a custody battle, or have been arrested for possession of a controlled substance—but the only reason they're standing before the judge is that the whole system is trying to fleece them, not because of any fault of their own. Addicts are capable of great justification if it means denying the consequences of their actions.

Mental illnesses like depression and anxiety can complicate matters further, whether as cause or effect. Sometimes a person uses because they're suffering from mental illness, and sometimes they develop emotional problems because of their addiction.

If I suffer from depression, anxiety, or bipolar disorder, I may be using drugs or alcohol to self-medicate. At first, I just take a little bit—some Valium or Ativan, maybe a little bourbon—to level me out. But eventually it leads me on to other things. Soon, I'm drinking so much bourbon people can smell it on me, so a friend turns me onto OxyContin. This is how self-medicating can lead to drug abuse.

On the other hand, I may have begun drinking to fit in, but because alcohol is a depressant, as the initial euphoria wears off, it causes depression where there has never been depression before. This depression motivates me to drink, to recapture that euphoria, and my drinking becomes an emotional crutch.

Justin has often talked about how his need for drugs became tied into every aspect of his life, and soon he couldn't function without them.

I was coming from a very insecure place, a place full of anxiety and self-consciousness. When I took the pills, they gave me this burst of energy and this nirvana state of mind. I may have problems, but my problems seem so far off in distance that I can't even see them from here anymore. Before you're really physically hooked; it's a psychological thing and you start believing this lie that the drug makes you a better person. People like you more. You can function better in society, professionally. You're able to talk to people—to girls—you never thought you'd be able to talk to. You start believing the lie that this drug does this for me. But pretty soon it turns into a need. You've got to have the drug, because if you don't have it, you feel more anxious. You can't go to your job without it now because you don't know how to work without having that extra boost of energy. You can't face anything without it anymore, because it numbs everything. You don't have to feel anything. If anything bad happens to you, you don't have to really face it. Then what happens is the physical part hooks into you, and so then you're fighting it on all those fronts and it's just impossible. It's become impossible to battle all of it on your own.

Many addicts experience cognition changes and memory loss, as I did. Even after decades of sobriety, I don't do time very well. Most people can tell you in general terms the history of their lives: "In '79 I was doing this, in '75 I was doing that." But I've lost that ability to do that; I can't remember whole years. Even to this day, I can't remember birthdays or anniversaries without writing them down. For some people this comes with age anyway, but even after sobering up, I have never regained that ability.

OPIOIDS—WORSE THAN ALCOHOL

The psychological effects of opioids and hard drugs are more severe and come on faster than with alcohol. Just the act of shooting up or snorting causes the drugs to hit the neurotransmitter almost instantly, creating immediate reactions and in many cases, advancing the user to the addiction stage quickly after that. Going down this road so fast makes the psychological effects that much more severe.

Alcohol is a terrible, destructive drug, but it can take decades to inflict the kind of damage that heroin can cause in a few short years. I see twenty-year-olds whose lives have already been ruined. And the difference is not just in terms of the depression or anxiety they suffer, but how fast they have been brought to their knees by their addiction.

A person might look back and say, "Wow, last year I was captain of the football team and now I live on skid row." Or, "I had a wife, kids, and a good job, and now I'm living in this little apartment with three other addicts, and it's only been six months."

The cost of these drugs will also drag a person down quickly. People become willing to sell everything, right down to their bodies. Imagine going from living a normal life to prostituting yourself in the span of a year. Imagine the effect on your sense of self-worth, your ability to trust, your sense of belonging. And these are people who didn't feel like they fit into society before they started using drugs. A drug addict soon becomes perfectly willing to rent their car out people who need it to sell drugs, prostitute, or even kill someone.

Here's a story about how low drugs can bring you in a very short time. "Malcolm" (not his real name) came through Haven House after having been an addict for a very long time. His long-suffering wife, tired of being ripped off and watching their money go up his nose, created a separate bank account that only she could access, and put their savings into it to protect what they had left.

Desperate for drugs, and knowing his name was not on the account, Malcolm went to the drive up of his wife's bank wearing a wig and a dress, disguised his voice, and tried to withdraw money with his wife's ID. By the way, Malcolm has a chiseled faced and is very muscular.

The image might be laughable, but the implication is not. This is a person whose mind was so diseased, who was so divorced from reality, who was so desperate to get high, that he put this plan together and thought it was a good idea. Malcolm told us this story himself—and this was not even his wake-up call. Things got worse from there.

You can remove the physical access to the chemical by putting a drug addict in a drug-free environment for six months, but the day you release them they will be using again. You have to address the psychological and spiritual aspects of the addiction to make a lasting change.

SECONDHAND DAMAGE

Paranoia, depression, and cognition changes don't only affect the addicted party. Everyone in the addict's life is affected by these changes, and the worse the addiction gets, the more damage it does to their relationships. But it's not just the relationships that are damaged, it's the people themselves. Anyone in close orbit with a drug addict will be fundamentally affected—and sometimes changed—by their interaction with that person.

Some parents of Haven House residents cannot accept the truth about their children. They have a thirty-five-year-old son who is a heroin addict. He's been in and out of jail since he was fifteen years old. They've contacted us to help him stop using drugs, but they're still telling us how wonderful he is, what a fantastic person he can be, and how brilliant he is when just given the chance:

"He was at this one job, but they just didn't treat him right."

"Wasn't he going to work high every day?"

"Well, that was a special case; they didn't understand how to work with him. You have to be gentle and explain things to him, and then he's fine."

They have a truckload of excuses for their thirty-five-year-old ne'er-do-well: He's lost every job he's ever had because everyone was jealous. His last girlfriend didn't work out because she never really appreciated him. He has to be in treatment for the tenth time because none of those other places knew how to take care of him. Mom and Dad have spent every nickel they ever saved trying to help him, but somehow nothing is his fault.

Sometimes a rift opens up between the parents in reaction to the addiction. While Mom is still enabling and making excuses, Dad may be saying, "I'm not helping anymore. I've had enough of this one." Now the drugs have not only damaged relations between child and parent, but also affected the relationship between husband and wife.

It's clear that Mom's perceptions have become warped by this situation—she's become an enabler. It starts early in their lives, when Mom is willing to run to school when Junior gets in trouble.

"Little Johnny is so smart. The teacher isn't handling him well."

"Well, ma'am, he was smoking weed out behind the school and trying to get the other kids to smoke it."

"No, that was another kid. He told me it was so-and-so who was actually doing that. They're just trying to blame him."

The excuses for Johnny's addictive behavior start early, and as time goes by, every time Johnny is caught, he blames others and convinces Mom of his innocence. Pretty soon Mom's paying all his bills, Mom's defending him to everyone, and at some point, she even drives over and brings him a little Valium of her own when he's suffering from withdrawal. She is worried that it's too painful for him when he's coming down, and thinks he just needs something to take the edge off.

I am using Mom as an example here, but make no mistake, it could just as easily be Dad. Either or both parents are capable of turning a blind eye and enabling their child. In chapter 3 I will talk more about enabling, and the ways in which family members deal with addiction, but I want to explain here how much damage this can inflict on the family unit and the surrounding relationships.

This behavior comes from a place of love. Mom and/or Dad wants to defend their child, support him, and love him to the best of their ability. I have met many of these people over the years, and they mean well. Nevertheless, they are killing their children by enabling them. And while Johnny is getting sick and ruining his reputation, the whole family is getting sick with him. Observers will see their friends going down this path and say, "For God's sake, stop enabling this behavior! You're killing him!" But they can't—or won't—see it.

I know this because I have seen it countless times over the years, and before that, it happened in my own family. My mother had a lifelong friend with whom she was very close. But this friend was a no-nonsense kind of woman, and she was critical of the way I behaved when I was drinking. One day they were arguing about something I had done, and she told my mother, "Well, your son's just a drunk."

In response to this statement, despite having known this woman almost her whole life, my mother refused to ever speak to her again. All the lady did was tell the truth, but my mother couldn't stand it. When my mother was on her deathbed, this nice woman called just to tell her she loved her, and my mother refused to take her call.

This is something I regret immensely. My addiction made my mother small and petty, and she let it cost her an important friendship. The whole time I was drinking and ruining my own life, I thought, "Well, at least I'm not hurting anyone else." But of course, I was. We addicts will drag down the people who love us until they finally extricate themselves from our lives.

PHYSICAL DAMAGE

While the psychological damage drugs inflict runs deep and can be the hardest to shake, the physical damage is also terrifying and severe. Drugs will affect your bodily functions in every way. Their effects on the heart, liver, kidney, brain, and lungs are well-documented, and even just recreational drug use increases the risk for cardiovascular disease and stroke.

Cirrhosis of the liver, hepatitis, and liver cancer are serious risks for anybody abusing chemicals, not just alcoholics. Your liver can't process chemicals fast enough when you are abusing them, so it becomes fatty, causing fatigue, pain, jaundice, abdominal swelling, and other problems.[4] You might also see damage to the pancreas, which can lead to pancreatic cancer.

In addition to the memory loss and cognition changes I mentioned earlier, heavy drug use can lead to brain damage. In alcoholics, it is called "wet brain," which in addition to memory loss and confusion can cause loss of muscle coordination and eventually death.

Prolonged use of stimulants can lead to damage or even destruction of the dopamine receptor cells that allow us to experience pleasure. If these are damaged or destroyed, a person's ability to feel any pleasure without the drug will be diminished, or even lost.

Hallucinogens can cause flashbacks, image distortions, and the sensation of seeing "snow" like static on a television set. Opioid use causes hypoxia, which deprives the brain of oxygen. This can

---

4 Dennis Lee, "Drug-Induced Liver Disease," Medicinenet.com, https://www.medicinenet.com/drug_induced_liver_disease/article. htm#what_is_drug-induced_liver_disease.

have both an immediate and long-term impact, as the effects are cumulative.

Every drug is different, and so is every addict. You could sit two people next to each other and have them drink the same amount or do the same amount of drugs for years, and one will have serious brain damage while the other will have only minimal damage. Just because you know someone who drank for years with negligible consequences doesn't mean you or your loved one will fare as well. There is no predicting how your brain will react to a drug.

Blood pressure complications are another big problem we see in people of all ages. Damage to the heart can lead to cardiac arrest and stroke. We also frequently see weakened immune systems in our program. We spend $20,000 a year on medical bills, and most of it goes to bringing people to the doctor to deal with colds and sniffles they can't seem to shake. When they come to us, people haven't been eating well (or at all). They've been ingesting chemicals, not sleeping, and interacting with other sick individuals for months, or even years. Consequently, their immune systems fall apart. Repairing this damage with good nutrition and healthy living takes some time.

Opioids can also cause major gastrointestinal problems—constipation and bowel obstructions serious enough to result in hospitalization, and even death.

Another huge physical problem caused by opioids is sexual dysfunction. At first the drugs heighten the experience of sex, but eventually they cause erectile dysfunction and other sexual problems.

DIRECT PHYSICAL DAMAGE FROM DRUG USE

In addition to the long-term damage it causes, drug use can also be immediately dangerous. An intravenous drug user may clean a needle and leave a tiny, invisible strand of cotton stuck to it. Oblivious, they'll stick it into their arm, and that little piece of cotton will cause an abscess. As a result of those abscesses going untreated (intravenous drug users are not quick to go to the doctor and don't take very good care of themselves), many addicts end up having to have big pieces of their arms cut out, or even having to have an arm amputated.

Drug users are susceptible to tuberculosis, and the sharing of needles and other risky behavior can lead to HIV in some cases. Unclean needles can cause pericarditis, an infection of the heart lining. And lest you think crushing opiates and snorting them is safer, this practice can cause a deviated and perforated septum, leading to nosebleeds and other painful issues.

DETOX

Using drugs causes damage, but sometimes stopping can be even worse. Weaning yourself off drugs can be a painful and even fatal experience. While detoxing, people find out the hard way that they are prone to seizures. Sometimes people have a seizure and end up falling and hitting their heads on the sink, crashing their cars, or falling down the stairs.

Even without seizures, coming down from drugs is a dreadful experience. (Remember Justin's description in the last chapter about detoxing from opioids?) In the first stage, people will experience high anxiety, depression, insomnia, nausea, vomiting, tremors, the shakes, heart palpitations, and more. The second stage will bring increased blood pressure, a rapid rise in temperature, mental confusion, the sweats, and mood swings. After about three days to a week you enter the third stage, which includes hallucinations, fever, confusion, and agitation. Sometimes the psychological effects can become permanent.

As terrible as opioids are, alcohol is one of the worst substances to detox from. Alcohol withdrawal has all the same symptoms, but carries the significant possibility of death for the most serious alcoholics. If you're coming off opioids you may think you're going to die—you may even wish you would die—but you'll survive. But when detoxing from alcohol, you actually run the risk of death, and so alcohol detox should be done with medical supervision.

This is to say nothing about the mental issues you experience when coming off the drugs. You're dying for another drink or another drug. You're just dying for one. You're reliving everything you did, wondering if it can be that bad, if it's worth living without it. The physical pain coupled with the high anxiety—realizing where you are, what you've done, and who's going to find out—is killing you.

IS THE DAMAGE PERMANENT?

Much of the physical damage described above can be reversed when a person goes into recovery. The sooner a person stops doing drugs, the better their chances.

But it must be said that there comes a point when damage cannot be undone. Everyone starts at 100 percent of their physical and mental potential, but when you begin to warp your mind and body with alcohol and drugs, you decrease that percentage, and it can be impossible to restore your potential. You might end up at 90 percent or worse. Whether i's memory loss, diabetes, heart disease, or cancer—whatever damage is done, some of it will be irreversible. You have opened a door that you will never be able to completely close.

As for whether the emotional and interpersonal damage can be undone, that is up to the individual, their family, friends and God. It comes down to how hard the addict is willing to work, how committed they are to change, and their capacity for forgiveness. It isn't ever easy, but I have seen miracles happen.

WHAT TO DO WITH THIS INFORMATION

I write this chapter not to frighten people, but to lay all the cards out on the table. It can be scary to face what addiction means, but it is important to deal in reality.

As disturbing as these facts may be, they will not be enough to scare an addict into getting clean. Addicts do not think rationally or consider long-term consequences. But it is important to recognize the damage as it is happening, and to know what to expect.

You can track the path of addiction by what is happening in the life of the addict. If knowing what might happen doesn't change an addict's mind, maybe it will inspire an enabler to change their behavior, to encourage their loved one to get help, and to stop being a negative influence and become a positive force. In the end, it might just save someone's life.

CHAPTER 3

ARE YOU HELPING—OR HURTING?

As a family member, friend, or even colleague of an addict, it is hard to watch them ruin their lives and wreak havoc in the lives of others. We have talked a bit about what addiction looks like, the path it takes, and the damage it causes. Now we need to talk about the very harsh reality of how you or your loved ones contribute to the problem—or at least, allow it to continue.

I want to be clear: *you did not cause the addiction, nor can you change it or cure it.* Nothing you did made your loved one an addict. As I mentioned before, a complex combination of DNA, life experience, and environmental factors causes addiction, and it cannot be pinpointed to one person's influence or behavior.

That said, how you react to a person's addiction may affect how long they are able to continue their behavior—and the severity of the resulting consequences.

SECRETS AND LIES

For addicts and their people, the tension in the relationship usually begins with secrecy. The lying, paranoia, and manipulation that come with hiding an addiction will create major secrets in a family, and eventually lead to trust issues. As an addict creates more and more of a double life, the family's trust deteriorates.

Eventually, you have to accept (often too late to avoid heartache) that you just can't believe anything they say. You're looking someone in the eye, someone who you know and love and who is supposed to love you, and you know they are lying to your face. It's an extremely frustratingly helpless feeling; there's no honesty, no loyalty, and no respect. When you come to this realization, it can create deep anger and resentment.

For other family members or siblings, there can be great confusion, and even jealousy. Increasing imbalances can cause indignation: "Why does Ben get to mess up his whole life, stay out all hours, not work, not go to school, and there are no consequences for him? Why am I working hard to do the right thing and lead a good life when he can do any old thing he wants and still you bail him out?"

Living with an addict can be very dangerous for everyone involved. An addict might violently turn on someone in the household for questioning what they're doing. Often drugs or alcohol will increase volatility and lower inhibitions toward violence, especially among people using drugs like alcohol, cocaine, crystal meth, crack, cocaine, or steroids. In extreme cases, out of their own increased frustrations, a loved one can be a danger to the addict, but in most cases, it is other way around.

When someone in your home poses a danger to the others, it is important to protect yourself and those who are vulnerable. Drugs change the people we love, and as hard as it is, we have to recognize when the trust is gone. Once they are willing to steal from their elders, or drive while impaired with their children in the car, willfully misplaced trust in them can prove disastrous.

This may sound obvious, but stop and think carefully about what you might be letting the addict in your life get away with. What are the signs you are ignoring? If you are not facing facts about what is going on right under your nose, you might be putting people you love at risk, and you are very likely enabling the drug addict in your life.

ENABLING

You have probably heard the term enabling before. Maybe you've even been called an enabler. It's hard to accept that you might be enabling someone when you know in your heart that you're just trying to help. But the truth is, most people don't know how to help people who are struggling with addiction, and their flawed attempts at helping end up causing more damage.

Enabling someone means you are giving them the authority or permission to behave however they want. Now, most people do not think that's what they are doing. They're not giving someone money to buy drugs and they're not encouraging them to use: "Ben knows we're not endorsing this behavior, so I'm not enabling him."

However, permission can be granted in many different ways. Even if you orally express disappointment in and disapproval of an addict's actions, what are you doing to make their drug use possible, even easier?

I have seen family members do all kinds of things that enable their loved ones to use drugs, all under the guise of "keeping them safe."

"If I don't pay her rent, she'll end up homeless."

"If I don't get him a car, how will he get to work?"

"If I don't give her grocery money, what will she eat?"

Enablers work very hard to minimize any negative consequences for their addict. There's always a sensible explanation or excuse for the actions of the addict. Loved ones will show up in court to explain to the judge how it's not really Ben's fault that he broke into grandma's house, stole her check book and emptied her bank account to buy drugs. Sure, grandma is broke now and might lose the house. But

Ben is actually a lovely, smart, and kind person. It's just the drugs making him act this way.

Drug addicts know what they are doing. They are going to make it as easy as possible for you to enable them, and they avoid the truth. Instead of saying they need money for drugs, they will ask for money to pay for gas or groceries. A rational person knows that this is a lie—an addict doesn't care about anything but the next high, and every dollar you give them will go to drugs. But the loved one refuses to admit that, and gives the money to them anyway.

Dad will begin to spin a tale about how groceries are so expensive, and despite working really hard, Ben only got fifteen hours of work this week, because the boss doesn't have full-time work to offer him right now. So, dad will go ahead and give Ben money for groceries. And he'll make sure the lease and the insurance on the car are both paid, and that the tank is full, because you know the job he never goes to anyway? He can't get to it without gasoline.

Justin has talked about how he would use his master manipulator skills to bargain with his girlfriends and turn them into enablers by withholding his time and attention.

"She would want to go to a movie and spend time with me, and I would tell her I didn't want to," he said. "Finally, I would haggle with her. 'I'll tell you what, if we can go by my friend's house, and you give me some money to buy ten Lortabs, I'll go see the movie with you.'"

Despite wanting to help their loved one, or simply maintain their relationship, enablers end up providing the money to buy drugs, the automobile, the fuel, and the insurance. By bankrolling the addiction or making the lifestyle possible, they're helping the person they love to die faster. We always tell them that—we look them in the eye and tell the enablers, "You're killing him." It's very hard to hear, and even harder to accept.

I have a friend who's a pastor (we'll call him Fred), who was dealing with an opioid addicted brother (we'll call him Jack). After years of worrying about him, Fred decided to buy Jack a house. His reasoning was, even if Jack couldn't pay the utilities, at least he would always have a roof over his head. Fred didn't see this as supporting his addiction—after all, he wasn't giving him cash to buy pills. He just thought, "This way, if I end up dying or something happens to me, at least he'll have a home that he can always go to, electricity or not."

It made sense on the surface. But it didn't take into account the depths to which an addict will go. What ended up happening? Once the deed was in his name, Jack turned the home into a flophouse for addicts. He managed to keep the lights on after all, because dope fiends would come over, pay him a little money, and shoot up on the premises. He destroyed the house—and ruined a peaceful neighborhood by turning a lovely home into a drug house.

Believe it or not, we also see a lot of enabling in the workplace, with certain kinds of bosses. Even people who you think would know better let their innate kindness get the best of them. I'm not saying innate kindness is a bad thing in general—it's a wonderful quality most of the time. But when you are dealing with a drug addict, they will sniff it out and take advantage of it for as long as they can.

The owners of a local car repair shop hire some of our "graduates." They are so supportive of our guys; they donate money to the program, and if we have someone who wants to work there, they'll make space for them and create a job. These are awesome, generous, selfless people, and they have made a huge difference in a lot of lives.

But at one point, one of our guys who was working for them started to behave differently. He was making all kinds of excuses and asking for his money in advance. To them it sounded reasonable. They were empathetic, and they really wanted to help, so they decided to advance him money. Then, he didn't show up for work, and they made excuses for him.

"Well, he said he was sick again," they said to each other, and slowly they fell into the trap.

They thought they were helping someone in need, but actually, they were enabling him to continue down a destructive road. Finally, after we intervened and explained what was really going on, they understood. We said, "If you let him go then maybe we can get him back in the program." That's exactly what they did, and yes, we did get him back in the program.

An addict will seek out enablers, and figure out how to best manipulate them. When a person won't enable them anymore, they move on to someone else. Justin, for example, as a young man, was able control his relationships so he could continue using drugs.

Girls want to help; they think they can fix you. You already know that going in, and you feed off of it. It's the same with parents. Your mother thinks she's doing things the right way because of her intrinsic ability to love you, but actually, you use it as a weapon. You use their desire to help or love you against them, just like you use every relationship against the person.

Again, so much of enabling comes from a place of love. It's love that drives a parent or spouse to try to minimize the negative consequences of their loved one's behavior, or an adult child of an addict to take responsibility for the parent's actions. The line between enabling and helping can be difficult to discern sometimes.

Do you ever feel like your love and concern are being used against you, almost like a weapon? Do you feel like your desire to help your loved one is being taken advantage of? In what ways are you making their life easier, and how is that affecting their drug use? Think carefully about the ways in which you are "helping" the person who is using drugs. It's very possible you are actually enabling them—and making things worse.

CODEPENDENCY

Sometimes, people come to terms with the damage they are doing and stop enabling. Other times, enabling is just a stop on the road to codependency. A codependent person needs to keep the other person sick, because they don't think they can function on their own. They generally have low self-esteem, and have become dependent on the other person to make them feel worthy, needed, and important. Eventually they will compromise themselves and give away their time, their health, their sanity, their money—everything they have, to keep the addict calm, settled, and content.

HOW CAN YOU TELL THE DIFFERENCE BETWEEN ENABLING AND CODEPENDENCY?

Like other stages of addiction, enabling and codependency are intertwined. There is not a clear trajectory from one to the other, and they can be hard to tell apart. Generally, enablers have been manipulated into it, or they're afraid the person will die without their "help." Codependents are invested, even if it's not consciously, in keeping the person sick and addicted. For a codependent person, it is all about control.

Remember our car mechanics who were just a bit too generous as bosses? That's a perfect example of enabling. They were making bad choices out of a sincere desire to help. They had no personal investment in keeping that young man sick, and as soon as we made it clear that's what they were doing, they stopped.

A codependent person would have refused to admit they were enabling, or that there was a problem. In their heart of hearts, a codependent person thinks, "If he doesn't stay addicted, he might get it together and realize he doesn't need me anymore."

A codependent spouse or a parent maintains their loyalty to an addict, consequences be damned. It doesn't matter what they've done, or whether the loyalty is reciprocated. Sometimes, I ask guys in our program, "How many of you have ever told your dad to go to hell?" They all raise their hands. "How many of you have said to your mom that you hate her, or you're going to kill her?" Almost to a man they raise their hands.

Still, some of these parents will go to the ends of the earth for their sons. They might be rotten, thieving, abusive criminals, but Mom and Dad don't care. They will support their kids to the detriment of their marriage, their jobs, and their relationships with their other children. They're so wrapped up in it, they might not even realize that their own self-esteem relies on it.

They will even go so far as to accept blame to ease the pressure on the addict. Fathers will say, "I wonder what I did? I didn't raise them properly." Or a wife will say, "If I were a better wife, he wouldn't be doing this." Or the husband will think, "I guess she's out doing drugs and sleeping with other men because I don't make enough money." They accept the blame for these insensitive, irrational actions, rather than placing the blame where it belongs. It allows the addict to continue their behavior, which keeps them in need of the codependent.

At the same time as they assume blame, codependents cultivate a sense of martyrdom, and they make it their whole identity. The feeling that they're helping and sacrificing gives them a false sense of self-esteem and even pride. "Oh, you don't understand what she's put me through. But, despite all the things she's done, I'm going to hang in there with her no matter what."

HOW DOES SOMEONE BECOME CODEPENDENT?

Just like with addiction, some people are predisposed to codependency. Maybe your father was a drunk and you began looking after him when you were just a kid. It's not just coincidence that you ended up married to a drug addict now. You've developed a need, a codependency that requires you to take care of someone. You need to put someone else's needs ahead of your own to bolster your self-esteem. Soon, the relationships you form are all one-sided; they are not about returning your love or forming a partnership, they're all about the other person. When your kids come along, one or two might turn out to be addicts as well, because it's grown into the family tree, and it's baked into the family dynamic.

People who are codependent with a drug addict might be aware and frustrated by these patterns. But the compulsion overtakes them, just like the compulsion to do drugs overtakes the addict. The codependent needs the drug addict as much as the drug addict needs the codependent.

Even people who lack the predisposition or understand the issues can fall into codependency. The strongest of people can succumb to it when it's their child.

WHAT DOES CODEPENDENCY LOOK LIKE?

The caretaker codependent person covers for the addict at all costs. In covering for the addict, they will often resolve their issues, whatever they may be. Just like the enabler, they will pay the rent and the foot bill. Maybe if they let the addict lose their car when it gets impounded, they'd never lose another one, but instead, they cover for them, and pay the fines.

When the addict is facing withdrawal, a codependent person "can't bear to see them suffer," so they will provide them with a little bit of alcohol, or drive them to meet their drug dealer. As the addiction progresses, so will the irrational behavior of the codependent person. Whatever it takes to maintain the status quo, they will do.

There is always an excuse, a "valid" explanation for why this time is different: "This time it really wasn't his fault and so I'm going to help him. He's really promised to change." It's just like when the addict says, "This is different. I'm only snorting these pills. I'm not injecting anymore. I can handle the snorting of it but I will never do needles again, I promise." A codependent person will always have a reason why this time is not as bad as before, why we can't hold it against them.

Here, the addict learns an important lesson:

"I can do it again. Nothing's going to happen. Mom and Dad have gotten me out of going to prison for the third time. What's to stop them from doing it a fourth, or fifth?"

Because of this, the addict doesn't face any natural consequences for their substance abuse. The Bible puts it this way: "Allow perseverance to finish its work, so that you may be mature and complete, not lacking anything."[5] But if folks don't face challenges and deal with the consequences, they remain selfish, self-centered children. They don't mature, because codependent partners or parents don't give them the chance to persevere.

I know a mental health professional who specializes in treating addicts. When I met with him not long ago, he told me that his son was in prison for the second time. "I don't know what to do," he said to me, and then he began reciting a litany of revealing actions he'd already taken, all exposing him to be an extreme enabler and codependent parent. This is a person who works with drug addicts, and despite being aware of the facts, he can't help himself.

The codependent dynamic is extremely detrimental for addicts, especially once they are on the path to recovery. To remain in those relationships without setting new boundaries is a constant danger, because the codependent parent or spouse does not benefit from their loved one's sobriety, and will be consciously or not looking to sabotage it. Mom, Dad, or the spouse need the addict to stay high and drunk.

This can make home visits for our fellows in recovery very hard, because the family dynamic unchecked or changed brings the addict back into the old pecking order and they are now at risk of using again. There's always a pecking order to a household. Our guys might be doing really well, but when they go back home, they are immediately thrust into that pecking order and become the middle child, the black sheep, the whipping boy, or the clown—whatever it is—and they begin to fall back into that role and fulfill it. It's that same role that led them to addiction, and now they're finding themselves back in the cycle.

---

5 James 1:4.

For this reason, we caution them never to live at home again—not even for a day. If they have to stay over during a visit, we tell them to be exceedingly careful, and if it gets to be too much, we tell them it's all right to, in fact imperative that, they leave. We tell them, "Love your parents. Let them be who they are where they are. Your job isn't to change them. But, you've got to be aware that the way you interact with your family is killing you."

ACKNOWLEDGING THE PROBLEM

It's possible to be ignorant of your enabling and codependent behavior. It can be hard to recognize, especially when you are trying to be helpful. But after a while, it becomes hard to deny the reality before you. Chances are, if you're reading this book, or you've come to Haven House and we're telling you that you're an enabler or a codependent, you've probably heard it before. If your spouse, sibling, or child has repeatedly lost jobs, been evicted, or been in trouble with the law, and you're still bailing them out, you might be in denial, just like an addict.

IS THERE SOMETHING YOU ARE REFUSING TO ADMIT, OR SEE?

You're not alone. Scratch the surface of any drug addict and you'll find a codependent family member, or enabler. That's why it is essential for an addict's family to go on their own journey of recovery at the same time the addict is in treatment. The steps for recovery are the same for the addict and the codependent party. Al-Anon is a recovery program created specifically for family members. It walks you through the steps and provides the same type of support that Alcoholics Anonymous and other programs do. The potential for change is there, and the resources are available, but too many people in this position refuse to take the steps.

The first step is admitting there's a problem that you can't manage. You have to make a "searching and fearless" moral inventory. But codependents are just like addicts. They don't want to do it. They are afraid of the big changes. What will the relationship look like without this sick interaction? They are afraid they will be abandoning their loved ones, or be abandoned by them.

One of the things that complicates recognition is that the codependent person is always professing their love for the addict, and how everything they do is meant to help them. But the truth is, a lot of it is lip service. Sometimes it's the codependent family member who forces the addict into treatment or has them arrested. But then it is usually only out of desperation because the situation is near death. They are not invested in any long-term recovery, not in their hearts.

Just like the drug addict who doesn't want to quit doing drugs, but wants the consequences of his actions to stop, the codependent wants the addict to avoid jail, overdose, and death. Yet, they don't really want to see the addict get better. We see this at Haven House, when people start making all kinds of demands.

It's amazing, the things we hear, even from the parents or spouses of hard-core drug addicts who are facing their last chance before jail or death.

"He's going to need these drops for his eyes. And he's got a little cough, so make sure you have this kind of tea."

And we tell them, "No, we have our own regimen. They get what we give them."

"Well," they will scoff, annoyed. "He needs [fill in the blank]."

Recently someone put their son in the program and then told me, "I've done his taxes and he's got to sign them, and it has to be turned in by this date and this time. So, could you go over it with him and make sure he signs here, here, and here? And then you can mail it to this address?"

Again, we say, "No. We won't do that. We'll give him the file and he can handle it himself. If he has any questions we'll help him find the answers, but he's going to learn to live on his own."

"Oh, that's horrible! You can't do that. You don't understand. He doesn't even know he has to pay his taxes."

"What do you mean he doesn't know? Everybody knows. America didn't have taxes before he got to the Haven House?"

These are the kinds of responses we give to try to shake them awake. Often it doesn't work. They get mad at us. They become frustrated.

"What have you all done about his asthma?"

"What asthma? He's fine."

"No, no. He needs an inhaler. You haven't done anything? You haven't taken him to the doctor?"

"No. But he's outside playing basketball, so I think he's fine."

"I've been bringing him those puffers since he was a little boy. He needs them."

"He likes taking those puffers that get him high, but he doesn't have asthma."

Some parents are suddenly very concerned about their sons' sex lives.

"Well, what about women? I mean, they've got to have women."

"No, it's not good for their sobriety at this stage. There are no women in the program and we don't arrange for them to meet women."

"Hmm. Then, I don't think this is for us because really he just needs a good woman and a job and everything will be fine."

Or suddenly their exercise regimen is very important.

"Do you have a weight room? He has to be able to lift weights."

"He can't exercise until we assess him physically."

"But this is part of his routine. It's essential he has access to a weight room."

"Was he lifting weights when he was living on the street, or strung out in the flophouse?"

There's a reason I'm providing so many examples of the kind of things we hear. If you are a codependent person, you are probably making excuses as to why you are different. You're already thinking, "Well, yes, but that's not us. My son is different. He really needs his vitamins, or women, or exercise."

But most likely, what he really needs is for you to not sabotage his treatment. Because when you make caveats or demands or concessions like these, that is what you are doing. You are trying to maintain control of the situation, even when your addict is out of your care. You are preserving what we call a sick relationship.

We see the symptoms of that sickness in our program all the time. On Sundays, parents are welcome to join their sons for church services. Sometimes, I'll sit in the back of the church and watch some of the mothers and sons interact. Moms will be rubbing their sons' back the whole time, or they will hold hands throughout the service. If you didn't know any better, you might think they were dating.

I'm not suggesting that anything physically untoward is happening, but it's clear that the love between mother and son has morphed into something unnatural and unhealthy. The codependency can lead to extremely bizarre and inappropriate behavior, very often to the detriment of the parents' relationship. The sick son starts to replace the husband as the main partner and confidante, or vice versa with fathers and daughters.

REWIRING YOUR RELATIONSHIP

People might not even be aware of how far they have strayed from the normal path. It can be quite a hike to get back on track, but it is doable. And despite the difficulty of the family dynamic, we never advocate the breakup of families in any way. But breaking the bonds of addiction requires work to be done on both sides.

We provide daily classes in which we talk about codependency and the family dynamic. We emphasize that, unless it's absolutely necessary, addicts need to stand on their own two feet, maintain their own lives, and face consequences for their actions. The key is to avoid the dynamic that has been a killer. We help both sides understand how to accept each other for who they are, and also set up appropriate boundaries.

All of this is going to be especially important for relationships with spouses, since the addict will likely want to move back home after the program. That's why the spouse also has to do the work and commit to a healthier way of thinking and living. We teach that it is important to establish good connections with your local recovery group, community, and church so that you have a place to go, an outlet when things get hard.

Once you are out of denial, happy endings are possible. This work is doable, but you must be willing to do it. You have to be aware of who you are and be realistic about your limitations. If you can stop enabling, and start really helping, the drug addict in your life will have a meaningful chance at recovery.

CHAPTER 4

STAGES OF RECOVERY

It takes a lot to get an addict to agree to get help. It would be nice if once a person agreed to treatment, it was smooth sailing from then on. Unfortunately, it doesn't work that way. Like everything else concerning addiction, the road to recovery is complex and difficult. But the good news is that there is a road.

You've probably heard of the twelve steps. Most treatment programs and facilities work with some iteration of the twelve-step model. What you may not know is that while an addict goes through the twelve steps, they are also progressing through the six stages of recovery: rebellion, recognition, admission, compliance, acceptance, and surrender.

As with the stages of addiction, everyone's experience of recovery is different—so while we review the general definitions of the six stages, remember that each person will reach these stages at their own pace, and not necessarily in the prescribed order.

REBELLION

If you've ever been a teenager, you've likely experienced rebellion. At some stages of life, a little bit of rebellion is natural, and can even be beneficial to maturity. Among drug addicts, however, this stage is serious and dangerous.

To some extent, addicts are rebellious throughout their addiction. People try to tell them they have a problem, but they won't listen. They're hiding from everybody, including themselves. When confronted with the truth, they deny it or become defensive. They project onto others.

"Look, you wrecked your car twice last month."

"So? What's wrong with that? People wreck cars all the time. Don't you remember when you had that accident? And you're pointing the finger at me?"

They practice this craft—denial, projection, and rationalization—until it becomes second nature. They must in order to live with themselves. And while they may hate themselves for it, eventually they also learn how to redirect that hatred toward others.

This is the rebellion stage, and it is not pretty. The truth is, most addicts die in the rebellion stage. They deny, obfuscate, and blame others for their problems, right up until they're in jail, dead, or even worse. I know people in their late forties who have ended up in convalescent homes where you would see mostly old folks. It's the only place they can live because they weren't able to maintain themselves. They have wet brain, poor health, and failing bodies, and they have to be looked after by professionals.

But if rebellion is the first stage of recovery, what does it look like in treatment? We see it all the time at Haven House—guys who are trying to work their own program. They are rebelling against the early steps, which involve admitting there's a problem, acknowledging a higher power, and relinquishing control of their lives.

An addict in the rebellious stage still thinks that they are the center of the universe. They think, "If I let go, my life will fall apart," when in fact, it's already falling apart.

Rebellion also means resenting everybody around us. Everyone who is trying to help us is wrong, and in fact, they are the cause of our problems. This is a persistent and insidious train of thought, and for a lot of addicts it continues through many stages. At Haven House, there are times when folks show up, and even though we've just met them, within a week of meeting us they decide we're the cause of their problems. They'd be sober now if not for us—never mind that they've been high for years. It's a real twist of logic, but that's where they end up after so many months or years of hiding.

CRISIS

The only thing that can break that rebellion is a crisis. Until something serious happens, addicts won't change. Some sort of calamity—possible jail time, a spouse threatening to leave, a lost job—is needed to shake them awake. Some people will only need to face a crisis once. Others will have to go through a hundred crises, and sometimes they still don't see the problem. But unless they experience a crisis that interrupts their lifestyle pattern, they'll stay in rebellion.

This is a juncture at which enablers and codependents can really interfere with recovery. If an addict never has to face a crisis because someone is always bailing them out, then they can remain rebellious forever. When I meet parents like this, I always tell them, "Well, listen, if you need another son, why don't you take me? I'll be drunk every day, but I'll cut the grass and I'll clean the gutters. At least you'll have a son who'll be doing something. And then you just take care of my fines and bail me out of jail when I need it, just like you're doing now."

Some get mad when I say that. They don't appreciate my dark humor. But sometimes that's what it takes to shake them out of their complacency. If you don't let an addict face crisis, they will never progress in recovery.

Alcoholics Anonymous calls it "a gift of desperation," and in some ways, it is a gift. The Bible tells us the story of the prodigal son, who asks his father to give him all of his inheritance, then runs away and wastes it all on wild living.[6] This parable is about debauchery, indulgence, and hubris—all things we associate with drug addiction and alcoholism.

In the end, the son finds himself feeding pigs for a living (not the most respectable job for a Jewish boy), so hungry that he's eating the pig slop to survive. The Bible says, "He came to himself." He experiences that crisis, and it gives him a moment of clarity. He realizes who he is, who he's supposed to be, what he is doing, and how off course he has gone—and off he goes home, where of course his father, God, is watching for his return each day, waiting for him with open arms.

When an addict is in the rebellious stage, that's all the families want—for them to turn away from that life and come home. In the end, they don't care what the addict did; all that is in the past. What matters is having that moment when you know things must change, and giving yourself over to that recognition.

---

6 Luke 15:11-32.

RECOGNITION

Crisis brings you to the recognition that there is a problem—and that's the entirety of the recognition stage.

Sounds easy, right?

Don't be fooled. The recognition stage may be short and simple, but it is also painful, messy, and incredibly difficult to get through. It's so hard that people often slide back into rebellion. Some people have to recognize the problem over and over again before they can move on.

Why is this stage so hard? Well, let's say you've been an addict for ten, fifteen or twenty years, and for most of that time you've been lying, manipulating, and cheating. When a crisis finally brings you to the recognition that there's a problem, it lays bare all the deficiencies in your spiritual and emotional life. There's a problem with your reasoning; your rational mind is a mess; all of your relationships are shot. Most people I see have become angry at God, if they still believe at all. I can't tell you how often I hear that everything they've done is God's fault. Years of conditioning have made it nearly impossible for them to learn from their mistakes, and it has become normal to deny, project, and rationalize.

Even your memory is not working correctly. By the end, the highs are far fewer than the lows. All you're left with is a desperate need to get high and avoid withdrawal. Still, you will cling to the positive memories and convince yourself that is still how it is today.

All of this makes it easy for a person in the recognition stage to slide back into rebellion. It just seems easier to revert to denial, minimization, and justification. In a sense, the novelty of recovery wears off. You cut back on visits with your counselor or attending meetings. You go less and less to church or synagogue. You're subtly shifting the responsibility of being the center of the universe back to yourself; once again you have all the answers.

This also happens because after years of substance abuse, an addict doesn't know how to handle emotions anymore. Eventually, when the real work starts, the guilt, shame, and pain are overwhelming, and in the recognition stage, you haven't yet figured out how to put that in order. You're only seeing it for the first time. When the reality begins to take hold—the realization of what you could have been versus what you are, what you could have done with your life versus what you've done with it—that can be enough to make a person crawl inside a bottle or put a needle in their arm.

And that's usually just the beginning. Addicts who are working to avoid their reality become prone to all kinds of wild behavior. Some go into criminal activity. Others are constant philanderers, even though their wives or husbands have stuck by them throughout their addiction. And then there are all the terrible things they have done to maintain their habit: Stealing from their kids' college funds. Taking loans out in their kids' names and getting them into all kinds of debt. I know people who have taught their children how to cook crystal meth—and then the kid ends up in jail just as Mom or Dad are hitting the recognition stage of their recovery, and it's yet another thing to come to terms with.

You'll often hear an addict claim, "I'm only hurting myself," even though they might be in a room full of people who are screaming and crying and tearing their hair out in frustration, pleading for them to get help. Moving from selfish to selfless is hard and to the addict seemingly impossible—the ability to feel for people, to prioritize others' welfare and emotions, are things you've had to suppress. It's difficult to retrain yourself and replace bad habits with good ones. This is how a person can live in the recognition stage for a long time.

ADMISSION

Once a person gets through the recognition stage, whether it lasts an hour or a decade, they have to accept that in light of everything, they've become unmanageable. Then they have to admit the awful truth about who they are and what they've done.

It's not going to be a one-day epiphany. Admission is a long process that requires honesty, humility, and a desire for change.

HONESTY

If you can't be honest with yourself, you're heading back to addiction. Most addicts have been dishonest for so long that this is the hardest part. Dishonesty is a habit, a defense mechanism, and it has become second nature. Addicts lie when the truth will do.

I remember talking to my brother once when I was newly in recovery, and I was just telling him the truth about something that had happened. I guess it had been a while since I had done that, because he said to me, "The truth is the best lie you ever told, isn't it?" And I thought about that, and in a way, it's true. The truth is so simple. You don't have to manage it; you don't have to manipulate it—you just tell it and walk away.

That is easier said than done when you've been denying your problem for ten, twenty, or thirty years. In that moment of acceptance, after you've told everybody in your life, "It's your fault," now you have to go back and say, "Hey, I was wrong and you were right. And by the way, I'm gonna pay you back the money I owe you."

Honesty is the key. It's the linchpin. That doesn't mean it's pleasant, or that we have to like it. We can do it angry. We just have to do it.

REV. CHARLES F. PLAUCHÉ

HUMILITY

Humility is no easier than honesty. Don't forget, it was our pride and ego that got us into that deep dark hole of addiction. And now we have to recognize our attitude, and somehow put it aside after we've relied on it for so long. And even as we are trying to get clean, there is still a little ego-driven voice speaking to us, deep within our minds, saying, *Hey, you know what? I'm gonna clean up, but I can still have a good time. No, I can't do heroin anymore, but drinking a beer or two won't hurt. After all I never got in trouble drinking. I know that won't hurt me.*

For some people, maybe that idea of harm reduction works. But this is very rare. Everyone else will find out the hard way that they can't ever touch any substance ever again.

It is that addict ego that romanticizes the idea that we're just a little bit different: "I know you guys can't do it. You may need all twelve steps. But me? I only need steps three, five, and seven. I probably can have a drink or two." Humility is a byproduct of facing the truth. So, if we don't get honest, we can never be humble.

DESIRE FOR CHANGE

Some people call this a desire for sobriety, but I call it a desire for change, because as we've noted, literal sobriety— just abstaining from alcohol and drugs—is not enough. We are talking about sobriety of mind and body. And to achieve that, we have to really want change.

When people come to Haven House, we don't care if they're happy about it. What we want to know is, today, do they know they need to change?

I say, "today," because I'm not worried about tomorrow. Families will say, "Well, he wants to change today, but two days from now will be a different story."

I don't care about that. When I interview them, I want to know if they're committed to change. They can be angry if they want to be. I tell them, "You can call me dirty names when I ask you to do something. Go ahead and call me whatever dirty names you know, and then go do what I asked you to do. If you can do that, then we can find some humility. Just enough, maybe, to move you out of the center of the world, and let God in where he belongs."

A powerful desire for change can smother thoughts like, I can have just one, or I'm a little different. Everybody has those thoughts, but the difference between the people who are able to overcome them and those who aren't is the desire for a change.

Desire will also keep you honest when the instinct to lie wells up in you. When your humility is waning it will remind you that you aren't the center of the universe. The desire for change is the touchstone that will keep you on track and disciplined.

Justin is one of my star pupils. He is talented and has a heart for helping others addicts. Justin had so much unbridled potential and commitment to service that we have hired him. He has come up thru the ranks and is now my right-hand-man and our Program Director. But back when he first went through our program, he was just another addict struggling to get clean. As he describes it, it wasn't an easy journey for him, but his desire for change was his northern star, and it kept him on the right path.

I went through terrible withdrawal, but I didn't care. It didn't matter to me how long it took. Anything was better than what I was doing. When I got to Haven House, it was two and a half weeks before I got any sleep. I had awful chills, sweating; it was one of the worst withdrawals I had ever gone through. But it didn't matter. I knew this was going to suck, but I was going to go through it. Whatever I had to do, I was going to do it. I was just done. It's a tough program, but for me, at the time, I was so done with that whole lifestyle, that the whole structure, the accountability, it didn't bother me. You've got to be honest, shave every day, be neat and on time. All those things: I didn't like them. I wasn't used to it. I didn't want to do it, but I did it because I knew what the alternative was. I just wasn't going back.

COMPLIANCE

Compliance is a tricky stage. On the outside, it might look like a person is on the straight and narrow. They've admitted to their addiction and are working hard to be honest, stay humble, and foster their desire for change. It would appear that they are sticking with the program. But we often see divided sentiments in compliance, and people often harbor inner reservations.

In the treatment setting, they are doing everything we want them to do. As Justin noted, there are a lot of rules at Haven House: wake up, clean up, shave, wear your hat straight, no baggy pants, be on time … but that's just the superficial stuff. On the outside, a person in the compliance stage might be doing all of this, but on the inside, there's some passive aggression.

Maybe they're only studying at half pace, or not doing the reading at all. It can be hard to live a life of discipline and service after being the center of your world for so long, and maybe they are having a hard time taking direction. So even though they are complying on the surface, they are finding little ways to rebel.

It may not seem like a big deal, but passive aggression is a slide back into old behavior. It means they're not being fully honest, they're not being completely humble, and they're letting something get between them and the change they desire.

Many people reach the compliance stage before fully going through admission. Maybe they're in treatment because they realize they'll lose their family otherwise, or they're facing time in jail. In some cases, maybe their life was at stake. So they are going through the motions, putting one foot in front of the other, but their heart is not fully in it. They are reluctant, and not altogether convinced they want this new way of life—it's new and it's scary.

Often, people in our program will arrange it so that we are forced by their actions to ask them to leave the program. It gives them a chance to say, "I was doing everything I was supposed to, but they threw me out. I was going along with that program, but it wasn't working." I know when I hear from someone, "I was in a program, but it wasn't working," something is not right. I say, "No, that program worked fine for you. You didn't work for it."

Sometimes you can tell when people are not making the switch inside, the commitment to inner change, because they are complying with all the requirements you can see and quantify, but are trying to fly under the radar when it comes to emotional and spiritual growth. When that happens, we warn them, "Don't think you're getting away with anything. We see what you're doing. We understand it, and you're on the edge." And we say it in a group setting in front of everybody, because after years of conning everyone, they think they can put one over on us all. But we are on guard for it.

When I was a young guy, still drinking, I used to ask my father for advice. Or at least, I pretended to ask him. I usually already had a pretty good idea of what I wanted to do, and my asking was a form of manipulation. So, my father would offer me advice, and I would be ready with a response. I would say, "Yeah, but … " And he would answer, "I know, Son, you don't want me to confuse you with the facts. You've already made up your mind."

True inner change is the only thing that's going to keep an addict from going back to where they were. In the compliance stage, we're like chameleons: we change our colors to match our surroundings, doing what it takes to fit in. But outward conformity has nothing to do with inward conformity. And those who don't conform in mind and body will return to chemical addiction.

ACCEPTANCE

In the acceptance stage, we take personal responsibility for our lives and behavior. That includes accepting responsibility for our past actions and our future recovery. There is an understanding that chemical addiction isn't the minor problem that we thought.

This is when we begin to truly understand the opportunity before us. Treatment programs, rehabilitation programs, Alcoholics Anonymous—they are all simply organized opportunities to help ourselves. I always tell parents who come to us, "We provide the vehicle, but sobriety is between your son and God. If he does well, that's his victory, not ours. If he does poorly, that's his loss, not ours. All we are doing is providing a successful organized opportunity for self-help."

This is the stage where it clicks for people that their attitude motivates action. They begin to understand that it's all about how they view things. Drunks and drug addicts tend to be emotionally volatile because they have no acceptance and they're afraid—afraid of life, afraid of loss, afraid someone's trying to get one over on them because that is who they have been.

But if we can accept life as it comes, we're not so volatile. We understand that if our attitude motivates and directs all our actions, we need to maintain a good attitude, an attitude of gratitude.

Part of acceptance is coming to this conclusion: "I used because I wanted to. Period. The boss didn't make me do it; my wife didn't make me do it. It wasn't because of my childhood trauma, or my tragic loss. I used because I wanted to use." Not that there aren't reasons we use, but the responsibility is ours.

Along with this acceptance, the door will open for real spiritual conversion. We can't have any real spiritual conversion until we know the exact nature of our wrongs. We have to admit to ourselves, God, and another human being, as the Big Book says, "the exact nature of our wrongs (sin)." Only then can we experience a real sense of forgiveness. Sometimes you hear people say, "Well, I'm doing all this, but I just don't feel like I'm forgiven. When will I feel that?" The answer is, "When you accept that you created the problem."

A lot of folks will swear they have made this conversion before this stage. But if they are not willing to accept that they're responsible for everything they've done, their newfound faith won't last. You can't have love in your heart and hate on your mind, so to speak.

SURRENDER

People think surrendering means accepting that they won't ever drink or do drugs again. But as we know, if you don't deal with the emotional and spiritual side, nothing will really change. True surrender involves surrendering our entire self to the care of God. Everything. We cannot be the center of the universe for any situation. It may start with the recognition that we have no power over chemicals of any kind and we have to stay away from them. But when you admit that you have become powerless, then who has the power? If the substance has power over you, does that mean it is most powerful thing in the world?

Remember, the Bible says, "When I'm weak, I'm strong."[7] That is because when I know I have something I can't handle, I can turn it over to God. God will handle it for me. When there's nothing I can do about it, when I can't win that battle, then I say, "God, it's yours." Now I can stay on the path and do the next right thing. I can behave like a person who may not have all the answers, but who has asked God for help.

Some twelve-step programs say you can't be willful. But you must be willing to turn your life over to the care of God, so there is some will involved. This tells me there's a good use of my will, and there's a bad use of my will. When we use our will for good, we turn more and more of our life over to the care of God, and pretty soon, we are spiritually fit human beings. Not perfect, mind you, but spiritually fit.

You may be choosing to turn your life over to God, but it is a choice you have to make over and over, every day. It's not enough

---

7 2 Cor. 12:10.

to take the bottle from the baby; we have to give up the baby who holds the bottle (or the syringe). We have to surrender that childlike mentality and become responsible for what we say and do. If we don't, we're on our way back, fast.

Alcohol and drugs are a symptom of an unsatisfied life. A person who isn't satisfied with who they are might find a drink or a drug that makes them feel powerful, and eventually they surrender to it. Make no mistake, addicts do understand surrender. After all, they have surrendered before. They have given everything—mind, body, and spirit—at the altar of substance, and look where it got them. Now they have to surrender to God to get back to the land of the living.

My nonreligious friends might have difficulty accepting God as the center. To them I just say, "How about let's start with surrender to G.O.D.: Good, Orderly Direction? Whatever you've been doing, do the opposite. Put the notion of order at the center of things, and as time goes by, maybe He'll change your mind."

Spiritual conversion is God's business, not mine. If I convert you or save you, as soon as I'm out of your life, you're lost again. My job is to try to get people started—get them to agree to surrender to something bigger than themselves, and provide them with a vehicle to get from here to there.

SOME GOOD NEWS

Something we say often in Haven House is, "The Good News is; the bad news doesn't matter." Because, the truth is, it doesn't matter what you did in the past—not in the last decade, and not last night. All that matters is what you're going to do today, and from now on.

Even once you're here with us, even if you've been acting up, giving us attitude, finding passive-aggressive ways to resist, when you decide to go straight, I don't care what you did up until now. If you are ready to put in the effort, we will leave all that in the past and head in a new direction with you. We won't hold it against you. So, when a guy comes in and is constantly troubled—but has a desire— we work with that, until he finally has his "aha" moment.

The Bible says, "As far as the East is from the West, so far has he removed our transgressions from us."[8] God throws your sins away, so the Good News is: the bad news doesn't matter. And we try to live like that.

This doesn't mean there are no consequences. If you are arrested for a DUI and it means paying fines, going to court, or jail time, then you have to comply. You may leave your past actions behind you, but the consequences may still be in your future. I always tell our guys, "If you've planted weeds, it doesn't matter how you change, you're not going to get watermelons. Weeds are still going to grow where you planted them, so you have to pick them, and plant better from now on. God loves you while you're picking those weeds, but you still have to pick them."

At Haven House, we provide our residents with structure, routine, and spiritual guidance. Through work and fellowship, we support addicts as they go through the stages of recovery and embrace the twelve steps as a way of life. We have found a blend of work, therapy, and worship to be an effective model for people struggling to overcome addiction.

---

8 Ps. 103:12.

CHAPTER 5

THE HAVEN HOUSE
APPROACH

I've painted a sometimes bleak but realistic portrait of addiction, the damage it does, and the process of recovery in general. Now I am going to tell you about the Haven House approach to helping addicts who are trying to find recovery and a new life.

Over the years, we at Haven House have developed a Christian-based twelve-step recovery program, providing individualized care based on biblical teachings, best practices, and the needs of each person. Haven House Addiction Recovery is a twelve-month program and the work, study, and recovery curriculum is intense and unrelenting. People who come to us have given their lives over to their addiction, and we are fighting to help them come back from the brink.

The twelve-step model of recovery is a time-tested method to help addicts find sobriety. The most famous twelve-step program is probably Alcoholics Anonymous. Most of us know it through popular culture, where it is portrayed as taking place in church basements and community centers, with members introducing themselves, "Hi, my name is So-and-So and I'm an alcoholic."

At Haven House, we take inspiration from that program and its main text, known as the Big Book. For many people, Alcoholics Anonymous (or Narcotics Anonymous, AA's twin organization for drug addicts) has meant the difference between life and death.

Yet despite its longevity and popularity, Alcoholics Anonymous is not going to work for everyone. For one thing, AA is based on daily meetings that last about an hour. One hour a day will simply not be enough for a lot of addicts, especially hard-core drug users. There are too many hours left in the day (twenty-three to be exact) to get into trouble.

People who find that the AA program works for them are those who can really plug into the community. They make friends, form social connections, and go to the potluck dinners, the dances, and the conventions.

But a lot of addicts are just not "joiners." They can't force themselves to be social, or seek out activities with other sober people. In the early stages of recovery, an addict is emotionally and mentally disabled, and they can't imagine how those activities could possibly be engaging or fun. To some people, they seem painfully hokey. Up until recently their whole idea of fun was to sit on the sofa and run needles into their arms and pass out. It's a hard adjustment, and it's easy to opt out if you're not a self-starter.

At Haven House, we start at six o'clock in the morning and we go until nine and sometimes ten at night. We are a community on the move, working, praying, socializing—together. We go on fishing trips, canoeing trips, walks on the beach, and all those things that make a life. They are built into the experience. We travel as a group, and as a result, our residents are rarely alone, and rarely need to motivate themselves to participate.

Discontinuing drug use is largely about replacing terrible, deadly habits, with different, productive, or at least neutral habits. But if you are only actively in treatment for one hour a day, it is hard to form new habits. Conversely, our residents are scheduled all day long, and there are rules about how they dress, how they speak to each other, how they work, how they make their beds, how they cut their hair. They are forming and practicing new habits all their waking hours.

At Haven House, there is little room to get into trouble. Your day is structured for you. In addition to twelve-step meetings, you're also provided with activities, friendships, and social interaction for about a year, getting you through that difficult point where you'd otherwise have to self-motivate.

One of the things you will hear in twelve-step programs is that if you are an addict, then you are an addict forever. Despite the fact that the literature says you can quit and quit for good, you will always, at your heart, be an addict. It is possible that some people benefit from that way of thinking. The struggle to stay sober and avoid drugs is real, and maybe hearing that at their heart they will always be addicted relieves them from the guilt that they still want a drink even though they haven't had a drop in six years.

But for other people—a lot of the people who come to us—this is a defeating notion. If you're always going to be an addict, if you can never say, "I've quit for good," then you're already beaten before you've even started. We encourage our residents to say that they have left the drugs and the lifestyle behind forever, and they're never going back.

Another way Haven House differs is in the way we deal with sponsors. We believe in sponsorship as a powerful tool for recovery, but we have a slightly different approach. In the old school twelve-step tradition, you were assigned a sponsor, but the practice has evolved to let the addict pick their own. As we've established, addicts are savvy manipulators who will seek out like-minded people, so choice of sponsor isn't always in their best interest. People entering recovery will scan the room and find somebody with similar, warped thinking, and pick them as their sponsor. People sometimes get the wrong sponsors at the wrong time and end up with the wrong advice.

That's why at Haven House, we have a group of volunteers, including some of our graduates, who come and act as sponsors. We have a lot of continuity, and our message is cohesive. Our guys know they are getting guidance from people who have been through the same program and experienced the same problems they're going through.

HAVEN HOUSE PHILOSOPHY

I have often said that our philosophy is that we're raising these men again, as if from childhood. Many of them are emotional and spiritual twelve-year-olds. We're trying to give them a foundation of functionality, to bring them to the emotional and spiritual maturity of at least an eighteen-year-old before we put them back out into the world. We're teaching them lessons that they didn't get. Even if they were taught these lessons, for whatever reason, they didn't understand them.

The book of Job says that God favored Job by putting around him a "hedge of protection."[9] I like to think that, thru God's grace, we provide that hedge of protection for our residents. Once they're with us, they're in a cocoon, and they are given the chance to mature and progress.

In our care, everything is part of recovery. Work, meetings, outside functions, church services: all of these activities act as therapy. We are training our residents to be functioning people in the world. And, since everything is done in a group setting, your progress and your failures are public. If you drag your feet, kick stuff, or mope around, everyone can see you while you do it.

A negative attitude is normal and expected as part of the rebellion stage, as I described in the last chapter. For a lot of people, it's part of the process. Now, imagine having that attitude, and going to meetings just once a day for an hour. How much progress can be made? How will you snap out of that anger and negativity?

AA is for people who can incorporate recovery as something they're doing as part of the rest of their day. Haven House is completely immersive—everything is a tool for recovery, including the way you eat, work, pray, interact with people, and listen to music. Everything's about recovery and building a new spiritual life.

INTAKE

We conduct a multistage interview before we accept someone into the program. They've got to talk to two different people before being accepted, so the decision is shared and balanced. We're trying to avoid personality conflicts and determine if we are talking to someone who

---

9 Job 1:10.

is really ready, who will fit it in, and who will benefit from what we do. It doesn't always work out for different reasons. If the answer is no, we'll help them find somewhere else to go.

For those who we do accept, we establish the tone of a highly structured, controlled, and disciplined environment from the very first phone call. A big part of what we are doing is akin to an intervention for the parents or the loved ones who reach out to us. It could be a friend, a spouse or partner, Mom, Dad, Grandpa, it doesn't matter—we start recovery with them.

During that first phone call, we often have to say, "You're killing them and you have to let them go. Here is why and how." We need to get that family member or loved one on the right page, out of that enabling mode, and into a really positive helper mode, or the this process is never going to work.

Sometimes, even parents and loved ones who are ready and on board are surprised by the length of time their sons will be with us. Not only is it a long stay, but they won't be able to call home or have any visitors for forty-five, sixty, even ninety days. Privileges are given based on each individual's progress, so it can be months before our guys call their parents. All of this reinforces the notion that we're very serious about our residents having their own space, and some independence away from the family. Everybody needs time to decompress.

When someone comes to us seeking help, we never ask them, "What religion are you?" or "Are you a believer?" We don't ask whether they are gay, straight, or indifferent. We don't care about the color of their skin, where they are from, or what their politics are. None of those things matter. What we care about is their desire for change. We ask them, "Do you know that you can't continue living the way you are living? Are you going to treat everyone here with respect, follow the rules, and commit yourself to change?"

CHANGING THE OUTSIDE FIRST

The first thing we do when we get a new resident is have him shave and cut his hair. I've got nothing against long hair; I have had a ponytail myself at various points in my life. It's not about personal style for our guys—we want them to see their faces in the mirror every morning. They can't hide behind facial hair and hair while they are with us—they have to see who they are every day.

It's also part of learning discipline. Every morning they wake up and shave, and they stay on top of keeping their hair trimmed. We also ask them to take out their piercings. This starts from the very first day and it goes for everyone.

I can't tell you how many of our men think we are kidding when we say, "You have to cut your hair." Some of them realize we are serious, and leave. The few who do would rather forgo recovery than cut their hair.

Do they really love their hair or beard so much? Probably not. It's usually a sign that they're not ready and they're using their hair as an excuse. Requiring them to keep a respectable appearance implies that this is a serious place with serious people and we're not going to compromise, even over the little things.

"You have to take your earrings out."

"But I've had these in for ten years, I can't take them out."

"So, you're willing to sacrifice a new life to keep your earrings?"

It seems like a crazy reason to sabotage sobriety, but I have seen people do it. They are just not ready to conform to the structure and order because it means everything is about to get real and a panic sets in. Sometimes they'll be in our office talking with their parents, about to check in, and they get aggressive, so we stop right there, let them know they can walk out the door. They're not going to get away with disrespecting people that way anymore, and everything has to change on the first day—the first hour—of the program.

One of the things we're trying to impress upon people is that they are committing to doing something, and sticking with it. I mentioned earlier that the Bible says that we persevere through trials to mature, to become complete. It is difficult, because on the whole, drug addicts and alcoholics don't persevere—they're quitters (in every way but one). Usually at the first sign of trouble, they give up, quit, and move on. They quit jobs, they quit marriages, they quit families, they quit everything: "I tried to stay sober, it didn't work, so I quit."

But how do you teach someone perseverance? At Haven House, we start with discipline when it comes to haircuts, shaving, and keeping their personal space in order and the uniforms that they wear to work. Shirts have to be tucked in, buttons need to be buttoned properly. If you have visitors, you want to put your best foot forward, so we expect them to be dressed nicely. To build self-esteem we must do estimable things. We start by teaching them some self-respect and respect for people they have invited into their home. We demand it.

STRUCTURE AND SCHEDULE

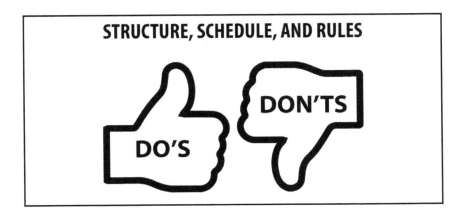

Haven House Addiction Recovery is a twelve-month-long program. Every day starts at six o'clock in the morning with prayer and meditation, and residents will be on time. For about a week or two, they'll have a big brother to help keep them on schedule and to show them the ropes, because their minds are a bit foggy coming off the drugs. Very quickly, however, it is up to each individual to make sure they keep their own schedule. They are grown men, and we're not going to tell them when to go to bed or when to wake up, but they know what time the first meeting starts, and they are expected to be there.

We have many different meetings. Morning meetings are different kinds of lessons and individual feedback sessions. In the evenings, we do a lot of our twelve-step work. There are sponsor meetings, reading group meetings, bible study, and other meetings that keep our residents engaged and working on themselves.

Before the morning meetings residents clean their room, make their bed, and organize their personal area. They'll all be assigned a chore, like cleaning a bathroom, mopping the floor, or dusting. Then they make their breakfast and get ready for the morning meeting. After that they're off to assigned tasks for the day.

Most residents work in our thrift shops. We have two community-supported thrift shops that provide work therapy and training for our men, serving as critical components to meeting the recovery program goals. Work therapy gives residents the opportunity to build relationships, learn new skills, work toward a common goal, and practice discipline and structure. Every resident has the chance to establish responsible work routines and ethics. By adhering to standards of accountability and punctuality, residents learn healthy habits that will aid them after they graduate. Residents learn how a small business operates in all phases. From mopping floors and cleaning the bathrooms, to scheduling pickups, to counting the money at the end of the day, our residents learn to become valuable employees and members of the team.

When they come home in the evening, they get cleaned up, the meal is prepared, and we all eat together. Then we clean up the kitchen and the cafeteria, and we're off to the next meeting—a twelve-step meeting, a Bible study, a sponsor meeting, a reading group— whatever the meeting is that night.

After that meeting, we have half an hour of quiet time that gives everyone a chance to go over their day, put things in order, and think about where they might have made mistakes. It's a very important time for our residents, and as they get used self-analysis, it becomes very a positive exercise for them. They learn about reflection and ownership, about how you can still get something out of an imperfect day, while striving to be better tomorrow.

Then we go to sleep. We don't give them a strict lights-out time, but they know they have to be up at six for the prayer and meditation meeting, so they learn fast to get some shut-eye at a decent hour. When we wake up, we do it all over again.

This is a general overview of the day-to-day operations, to give you an idea of how structured, disciplined, and full each day is. We don't give our residents a lot of room to get into trouble, but we do give them a lot of opportunities for inner reflection.

RULES

For the first three to five months, there are no phone calls to anyone, including family and loved ones. As they show progress, our residents gain more and more privileges, including access to a phone. At first, they can only call their sponsors. Eventually they can call home.

We do not allow personal cell phones at Haven House. One of the worst things you can do to someone's sobriety is give them a phone. They'll be calling girlfriends, boyfriends, drug dealers, enablers—it's chaos.

After about two months, we'll allow residents to have visitors. Again, the timeline depends on personal progress and is different for everyone. When families do visit, they come for Sunday service, and then have a meal.

After about five months, they'll get a pass to leave the grounds with their families. Passes will progress from eating lunch in a restaurant after church, to getting overnights at home every two weeks. Sometimes we'll have to rescind a pass, either because their behavior is slipping, or someone in the family is having a negative effect on them.

There will always be some aggression among a group of men with addictions. A certain amount of anger is expected, and we are ready for it. However, we have zero tolerance for physical aggression at Haven House. Consequently, in the more than the two decades we've been helping people, we've never had a fistfight on campus.

SPIRITUALITY

In our Bible studies, we look at the practical lessons the Bible offers us. It's an important part of the work we do at Haven House. However, spirituality is not limited to study sessions and church services. It is a part of every activity and every day.

Every aspect of the program is set up to instill discipline, and we believe in biblical principles. The last attribute of the fruit of the spirit is self-control. We are helping our residents develop self-control for the first time in their lives, so every time they make their bed, tuck in their shirt, or show up to work on time, they are living out Christian values.

A lot of our guys have been told that they're going to hell, and that they're bad people who'll never do any better. If you hear that enough times, you start to believe it, and it becomes a self-fulfilling prophecy. We are giving them practical lessons from the Bible that will help them create order in their lives and give them hope. We are also helping them get out of the center of their own lives and put God back where he belongs.

How does making your bed add to your spiritual life? The Bible says, "But all things should be done decently and in order."[10] How does showing up to work help you find God? "Whatever you do, work at it with all your heart, as working for the Lord, not for human masters."[11] How does keeping busy and filling your day add to your faith? "A sluggard's appetite is never filled, but the desires of the diligent are fully satisfied."[12] And don't forget, "Idle hands are the devil's workshop" (although this is not found verbatim in the Bible).

---

10 1 Cor. 14:40.

11 Col. 3:23.

12 Prov. 13:4.

If we take the time to look, the Bible has directives and guidance for every aspect of our life.

Beyond the specifics of verse, a peaceful, calm mind is essential to recovery. We try to teach people to be content and satisfied right where they are. Part of the addiction is the excitement and the unpredictability—an addict's life is full of drama and adrenaline. Eventually, they are as hooked on the chaos as much as the drugs. Getting them to sit still is difficult. When the turmoil isn't there, they don't know what to do.

We are trying to teach them a low and slow life. For some, our days seem boring or monotonous at first, but they need to be able to find satisfaction in the uneventful. They need to be able to take their own immature desires, personal entertainment, and instant gratification out of the equation. By creating order and establishing the presence of a greater power, they are answering to someone other than themselves.

AFTER HAVEN HOUSE

After they are done with the program, many men move back home. They are not resuming their lives, but building new ones based on their new foundation of discipline and spirituality. However, some men are not ready to go back to the world just yet. Some of them stay for a few extra months as part of our Give Back Program. It is an opportunity to branch out, while still remaining in a safe and supportive environment.

The Give Back program allows residents to stay for a couple of months, get a job, and save money while supporting Haven House. The purpose is to help the new graduate get established and for the new graduate to give back to the program by supporting our new residents. The graduate pays Haven House $600 a month for their share of expenses, and when they are ready to go out on their own, we give that money back so they can put it toward their new apartment. The graduate gives to Haven House and Haven House gives to the graduate—this is the essence of the Give Back Program.

We also have a Leadership Training Program. If someone is a good fit, they will work for us for four to five months, with increasing responsibility. We will assign them staff to start teaching them how to lead. With fifty thousand square feet of campus and stores to operate and maintain, there are many learning opportunities for the men. We love to be able to instill trust and responsibility into our graduates who know the culture of the organization, and they get a confidence boost and a learning opportunity. We are doing what we can to give these men a good running start.

COST

At Haven House, no one is turned away because they don't have money. If you're a good fit but don't have any money or anybody who can help you, we'll take you anyway. That said, the whole program costs about $25,000 a year per man, so we do need people to pay when and what they can. We've set up a sliding scale from something to nothing. We find that people who can afford the program are happy to pay, and often donate beyond the cost, so somehow it all works out.

WHY MEN ONLY?

You've probably noticed, when I speak about Haven House residents, I am only speaking about men. Obviously, women can also be drug addicts, so why is our facility for men only?

The reason is simple: for men who are trying to recover from addiction, the presence of women is not helpful, and vice versa. Think about what that would be like: You've ruined your life up until now. Here you are in this program, where you don't know anybody. When you look around the room you notice a woman who you think is cute. You think, "If I could get with her just for a little while, I would feel so much better." If you can think about her and obsess about her, you don't have to think about yourself, everything you've done, and what it's going to take to get back to normalcy.

Women in treatment are thinking the same thing—that's why treatment center romances are notorious. It happens all the time, and the odds are stacked against it ever working. Often, both people end up in worse shape than before.

At Haven House, we keep it simple: no women. Not because women are bad, but the passion, distraction, and irrational feelings that come with romantic entanglements are unproductive for anyone who is trying to get their life back on track. Someday we would like to open a women's facility and expand our reach, but even then, we will be keeping the two facilities separate.

There is much more I can tell you about what we do at Haven House—our philosophies, our methods, and our history. I have many anecdotes to share, both success stories and cautionary tales. I hope this has served to give you a general overview about who we are and what we believe. We have been able to help many men find a new spiritual life and new path. If this sounds like a program you or your loved one might benefit from, please contact us and we can begin to figure out whether we can offer you some hope in these dark times.

CHAPTER 6

WHAT NOW?

In the introduction to this book, I wrote that if you are concerned that you or someone you love is an addict, chances are you're right. After all, how often do you hear about that suspicion being wrong? "I thought Jake might be addicted to pills, but it turns out he's not," doesn't happen often. If you are looking for advice because you suspect there is a problem, you probably already know, on some level, that you are dealing with an addict.

After you acknowledge the problem, the next question is, "What's the severity of the problem?" Sometimes, if you notice someone is drinking too much or overdoing pills, you have to look at the whole picture. Is it possible this abuse is new, brought on by recent events or emotional changes? The economy, divorce, death— there are many situations in which people use drugs and alcohol as a crutch. It's never a good or healthy coping mechanism, but it is not always an addiction. Is this habit new, or has it been an on-again, off-again thing since they were young?

Sometimes you can be honest with a person, explain you are concerned, and they will hear you:

REV. CHARLES F. PLAUCHÉ

"You got really sloppy at that party last night."

"You're right. I need to lay off the booze for a while."

Have you already said something to them more than once? Have you set ultimatums, but not followed through? If they are ignoring your concern, if this has been occurring for years, if it's a crutch they take advantage of at the slightest provocation, then it's likely a bigger problem.

I knew someone who had lost his young son. It was a tragic, random turn of events, and he was really struggling to cope and drinking to excess. I said, "Well, if he crawls into a bottle for a while I don't blame him." It wasn't a lifelong struggle to fit in or a built-in codependent family dynamic driving him to addiction. It was a momentary problem caused by trauma, and I knew eventually he would come out the other end.

On the other hand, what if seven years later, he was still doing it? That would have signaled a larger issue, a sign that a door had opened and exposed deep-seated problems.

Once, I had a phone call from someone asking for help. He said that ever since he'd had a procedure done in the hospital, he had been hooked on prescription drugs. I went over to his house and had a look around.

"You don't have a problem," I told him.

"What do you mean? I'm eating Percocet like candy!"

I brought him over to the mirror and I pointed to the tube coming out of his back. "You have a tube coming out of your kidney. Take all the medication you need for now. When the doctor removes the tube, if you still have a problem, call me back."

Sure enough, when they fixed him up and the tubes came out, he quit the pills within a week. This is one, rare instance in which someone suspected a problem, but was wrong. That is not to say he couldn't have become addicted—for many addicts a trip to the hospital is exactly where it starts.

With every person, you have to look at the specific circumstances and trust your gut. You have to be willing to admit when something is not right, when it's a bigger problem than you can handle alone.

GET OFF THE FENCE

The man who called me because he was worried about his pill intake did the right thing. It would be a better world if everyone exercised this kind of caution. It's rare to think there is a problem when there's not, because it's usually the opposite situation: people will avoid the truth at all costs.

One of the things that is so scary, that keeps people from admitting there is a problem, is the stigma attached to drug addiction and alcoholism. In recent years, it seems to me that the stigma is lessening, but there is still a lot of shame and guilt associated with addiction. People will stay silent, thinking, "If people know he's gone to recovery, he'll be humiliated. It will ruin his reputation."

In fact, by trying to protect the addict, they are prolonging everyone's misery. Here's the truth for the family members: if your loved one won't get help, you need to cut them loose. Only by letting them go can you take care of yourself emotionally and spiritually. Then, when that person finally is ready to make a change, you will be emotionally, spiritually, and financially fit to help them. I try to make this clear to our enabling parents, because if they don't become emotionally and spiritually fit, they will be no good to anyone.

Whenever an addict goes further and further down the rabbit hole, his enablers descend with him. They spend all of their personal, emotional, and spiritual resources. When the addict is finally ready and wants to get help, the people they turn to no longer have any money, patience, or energy.

When I tell someone that they need to cut an addict loose, I'm not only speaking about cutting off the flow of money. Letting them go means giving them no childhood bed to crash in overnight, no home to shower in when they've been on the streets too long, no grocery money when they're hungry, no bail money for jail. If your son or daughter is living in a flophouse, but comes home now and then for a bath and a home-cooked meal, you are enabling them. You are contributing to their drug ritual. You are not helping.

I know this sounds harsh, but you have to stop sitting on the fence, and commit yourself to being part of the solution. I have two little girls, and if—God forbid—one of them became an addict, I think what I would do is cut them off, and then cry every day. If you have to do this, you will cry. You will feel guilty and terrible and miserable. But will that be worse than seeing them in jail, or burying them?

I'm not saying it's going to be easy, or that you'll feel good about it. I'm not even saying I know for certain what I would do in that situation. I'm just saying I know what is right, and what is most likely to work.

Putting off recovery damages everyone. When I am in a room full of addicts, I'll say, "How many of you know people who have died from their addiction, either through drug-related illness, crime, or overdose?" Inevitably, every hand in the room goes up. That's what comes from waiting.

IS MY SITUATION RIGHT FOR HAVEN HOUSE HELP?

In chapter 5, I talked a bit about Haven House—our philosophy and our methods. What we're doing is difficult, and it will not work for everyone. We take in people who really want to get sober, and already have a burning desire. If you don't have that willingness to change, you are not going to fit in with our residents and program.

Everyone who comes to us is working hard to change their life, to build spirituality, and to acquire discipline and purpose. They will not tolerate someone who is not going to fight for himself, because they know it's easier to drag somebody into the darkness than it is to pull them into the light. They won't be willing to risk their own recovery.

Most of the time, if someone doesn't fit in with us, it's because they're just not ready. We can tell because they balk at our rules right away; they don't want to cut their hair or shave their beard. They begin to tell us why we're wrong about what we're saying, and they explain what we need to do to help them. As I said, we expect a bit of this resistance from everyone; it's part of the rebellion. However, there are some people who just won't give in, even when it becomes clear we are not going to bend to their will, even when their very lives depend on it.

Sometimes it's the parents or loved ones who are not ready. We often feel resistance from parents who have been trained to enable, or who are locked into codependency. I've had parents say, "Well, what is he going to do for sex for a year? If you don't let in women, how's he going to have sex?"

If someone is more worried about their son's sex life than his spiritual and emotional life, they should probably look for a different program. If we continually find roadblocks being thrown up by family members, it sometimes means we don't have a good fit.

Sometimes there is a physical or medical condition or need that prevents us from helping someone. We just don't have the facility for certain individuals with dual diagnoses or ailments that require constant monitoring. For example, if a person has a heart condition and needs to see a specialist once a week, it's simply beyond our scope.

Also, people with certain legal problems may have needs that are outside of our capacity, so we require all legal problems to be sorted out before entering the program. We cannot cater to individuals with ongoing legal issues that require multiple court visits or a community control sentence that requires a check-in twice a week.

Residents sometimes arrange to work around legal problems. For example, a person facing charges might take it upon themselves to approach the DA and ask, "If I go into treatment, will you forgo the charges until I get out, or find me guilty now and let me go to the program instead of jail?"

That being said, we aren't working directly with the court system, and no one is mandated to enroll in our program as an alternative to jail. Occasionally we take in people who are on basic probation, with once-a-month reporting, but we usually help them arrange for write-in or call-in reporting so that they don't have to be there in person. These cases are usually associated with minor charges, not violent offenders.

Some candidates aren't a good fit, but we still believe they need and deserve a chance at recovery. We try to help everyone find a place where we think they will succeed. We'll assess the person and the situation, and we'll try to plug them in somewhere they belong.

WHAT WILL IT BE LIKE WHEN I ASK FOR HELP?

It's rare that the first phone call we receive is from the addict himself. The first point of contact is usually a parent, grandparent, or a spouse trying to find help. First, we will ask some questions about the current situation: Where is he staying? Does he have a job? How's he getting around? How's he paying his cell phone bill? The answers to these questions will give us an understanding of the situation at home, and help us determine whether an intervention is required.

The intake process is overseen by Justin. The initial work is done on the phone. We sometimes we will spend days, weeks, and even months intervening on the phone, trying to help parents and loved ones do what needs to be done.

"I tell them, 'You love him so much that the only option, the only way you're going to help him, is to get him help,'" says Justin. "I say, 'You're done with the enabling. You're done with paying for things. You're done with having them in your house. You're no longer paying for his cell phone bill, and his car, and his gas, and you're not going to listen to his ranting either.'

"Sometimes they'll call me back two months after I spoke to them and say, 'You know what? You were absolutely right. Now he's in jail with a DUI, or he's racked up theft charges. I wish I'd listened to you before.'"

The next step is to have the addict himself fill out the application. We tell them to take their time and answer everything fully and honestly to give us the best opportunity to accept them into the program. Sometimes they have to redo it several times.

"I want to see their willingness, their ability to listen and follow instructions," says Justin.

Then there are more phone calls, more conversations. We will push them a little bit on the phone to observe their attitude, how easily they get angry, whether they are glib or ready to talk back. If we're unsure about someone, we'll tell them to call us back the next day at noon. Once I had a man call me every day for a week. Finally, when I decided to accept him into the program, I told him, "Be here in an hour," and he jumped at the chance. That man ended up working for us for more than a decade and was an integral part of our beginnings.

Finally, we will schedule a day for the addict to arrive at our facility. There is no "checking out the program" or "touring the grounds" first. He comes ready on the designated day, with his bags packed, and moves in immediately. If someone asks, "Can I tour the property first?" or "What kind of food do y'all serve?" that's a sign. We immediately tell them, "You're not ready. If that's what you're thinking about, you're not ready to be here."

The truth is, our food is amazing and our facility is wonderful (check it out at havenhouse.net), but that's not the point. If they're asking those kinds of questions, they're not desperate enough, and if they're not desperate enough, then they won't be willing to do whatever it takes to get the help they need.

When they arrive to check in, we review everything discussed in the initial calls. The rules are restated. Their attitudes are noted. We check one last time for pushback. Then, on that very same day, they get a haircut, shave, and uniform, and they enter the program immediately.

I am describing our intake in some detail, because if you are going to contact Haven House (and I want you to contact us if you think we can help), you should know what to expect. All these steps are to make sure that the men who come into our program understand they need to change, are going to fit in with the others, and have the best chance to succeed.

LET US HELP YOU

I used to have a late-night program on a local public access station. It wasn't exactly prime time, but I knew the time slot would be effective for the people I was trying to reach: those who were on a bender, or at the end of a three-day run, and were unable to sleep. I knew they'd be up watching television in desperation, looking for something.

At the end of the show I would say, "If we can help you, call us and let us help you. If you can help us, call us and help us." No matter who you are, sometimes you're the person who can offer support, and sometimes you're the person who needs it. I know that better than anyone—I've been on both sides of that equation.

If you have recognized yourself or someone you love in these pages, chances are you are in need of help right now. Maybe until now you have been trying to convince yourself that it's not as bad as it seems, or that the people who have been warning you were overreacting. Maybe you've convinced yourself that some of this behavior is normal, that everybody does it. But now is the time to face the facts: you need help, and finding that help today is better than waiting until tomorrow.

Throughout this book, I have tried to keep things very simple and clear. I have been straightforward about what addiction is, what it looks like, how you might be contributing to the problem, and how you might help hasten recovery. By being open about my own history of alcoholism, and referencing Justin's story of opioid addiction, I have tried to illustrate how a person can sink to the depths of addiction and still find a way out of it and into the light.

You may be thinking, "You make it sound so simple, but it's not. My situation is difficult and complicated." It's true, there are many complexities in every individual's story, and each addict is on their own journey, with their own specific challenges. This is true for all people, in both addiction and recovery, but it is not an excuse to remain on a destructive path.

An addict's justifications and excuses do not make them special. If the stages of addiction and recovery teach us one thing, it is that addiction is almost always the same at its core. It afflicts the same kind of people regardless of race, religion, or economic status—those who feel like something is missing, like they just don't fit in. It follows the same downward trajectory, and it requires the same work to escape. Therefore, each person's details may be unique, but the prescription will be the same: take yourself out of the center of your own universe, give in to God, and find the humility and will to get sober.

There is a crisis in America, and we all know about it. For some people, it's just another item in the news. However, for many people—like you—the crisis is urgent. It is in your home, in your mind, and in your heart. You are not alone. Many people are experiencing what you are going through; many have gone through it, and come out the other side. There is a path to a happy, healthy, drug-free life for you and your loved ones. You did not cause your loved one's problem, and you cannot fix it by yourself, but there are things you can do.

If there is one hope that I have for you, reader, it is that when you turn the last page of this book, you will pick up the phone, or turn on your computer, and ask for help. Whether you contact Haven House or some other program doesn't matter. All that matters is that you reach out to someone today. The next step is yours to take, and if you do it now, you may save someone's life. God Bless.

ABOUT THE AUTHOR

Reverend Charles Plauché is the Senior Pastor of Haven House Mission Church. Victorious over addiction himself, Pastor Charles has dedicated his life to working with the chemically addicted. As Founder of Haven House Addiction Recovery in Santa Rosa Beach, Florida, Pastor Charles has developed a unique "handmade" program of recovery based on three basic Christian principles: rescue, restore, rebuild. For over twenty years, Pastor Charles's unique teaching ability has led many to the light of a new life. And twenty years later, Pastor Charles is still guiding staff members to excellence and working one-on-one with students to find freedom from bondage.

Haven House Addiction Recovery